Science Behind Sports

Ice Hockey

Science on Ice

By Barbara M. Linde

Portions of this book originally appeared in *Ice Hockey* by Anne Wallace Sharp.

LUCENT PRESS

Published in 2018 by
Lucent Press, an Imprint of Greenhaven Publishing, LLC
353 3rd Avenue
Suite 255
New York, NY 10010

Designer: Seth Hughes
Editor: Vanessa Oswald

Cataloging-in-Publication Data

Names: Linde, Barbara M.
Title: Ice hockey: Science on Ice / Barbara M. Linde.
Description: New York : Lucent Press, 2018. | Series: Science behind sports | Includes index.
Identifiers: ISBN 9781534561137 (library bound) | ISBN 9781534561144 (ebook)
Subjects: LCSH: Hockey–Juvenile literature.
Classification: LCC GV847.25 L56 2018 | DDC 796.962–dc23

Printed in the United States of America

CPSIA compliance information: Batch #BS17KL: For further information contact Greenhaven Publishing LLC, New York, New York at 1-844-317-7404.

Please visit our website, www.greenhavenpublishing.com. For a free color catalog of all our high-quality books, call toll free 1-844-317-7404 or fax 1-844-317-7405.

Contents

Foreword

When people watch a sporting event, they often say things such as, "That was unbelievable!" or "How could that happen?" The achievements of superstar athletes often seem humanly impossible—as if they defy the laws of nature—and all sports fans can seemingly do is admire them in awe.

However, when a person learns the science behind sports, the unbelievable becomes understandable. It no longer seems as if athletes at the top of their game are defying the laws of nature to achieve greatness; it seems as if they are using the laws of nature to their fullest potential. This kind of knowledge might be thought by some to take away from a pure appreciation of sports, but that is far from the truth. Understanding the science that makes athletic achievements possible allows fans to gain an even deeper appreciation for athletic performances and how athletes use science to their advantage.

This series introduces readers to the scientific principles behind some of the world's most popular sports. As they learn about physics concepts such as acceleration, gravity, and kinetic versus potential energy, they discover how these concepts can be applied to pitches in baseball, flips in gymnastics, dunks in basketball, and other movements in a variety of sports. In addition to the physics behind amazing plays, readers discover the science behind basic training and conditioning for different sports, the biology involved in understanding common sports injuries and their treatments, and the technological advances paving the way for the future of athletics.

The scientific concepts presented in this series are explained using accessible language and engaging examples. Complicated principles are simplified through the use of detailed diagrams, charts, graphs, and a helpful glossary. Quotations from scientists, athletes, and coaches give readers a firsthand perspective, and further research is encouraged through a detailed bibliography and a list of additional resources.

Athletes, sports fans, and budding scientists will get something important out of this series: information about how to exercise and fuel the body to excel in competition, a deeper appreciation for the history of their favorite sport, and a stronger understanding of how science works in the world around us.

The worlds of science and sports are not as far apart as they may seem. In fact, sports could not exist without science. In understanding the relationship between these two worlds, readers will become more knowledgeable sports fans and better athletes.

Chapter 1

Hockey: A History

Fans are in the stands at a large indoor arena. The floor below is coated with thick, smooth ice. Players, some skating as fast as 36 miles (57 km) per hour, whiz by, all chasing the puck, which is traveling at about 100 miles (161 km) per hour. They rush toward a net at one end of the ice. A player wearing thick, protective padding is defending the net. A player from the opposing team slams the puck with a long, curved stick. The puck avoids the goalie and makes contact with the net. Some members of the crowd cheer wildly, others groan, and others boo. Welcome to ice hockey, the fastest contact sport in modern history.

According to the *English Oxford Living Dictionaries*, ice hockey is "A fast contact sport played on an ice rink between two teams of six skaters, who attempt to drive a small rubber disc or puck into the opposing goal with hooked or angled sticks."[1] Players must be top-notch skaters, have a high level of endurance, and be in peak physical condition. Legendary player Wayne Gretzky said, "Hockey is a unique sport in the sense that you need each and every guy helping each other and pulling in the same direction to be successful."[2]

Historians are fairly certain that ice hockey evolved from earlier ball-and-stick games played by various indigenous people—although not all of these games were played on the ice. For example, drawings on ancient Egyptian tombs show men hitting a large ball with long, crooked sticks. Similar drawings and carvings have been found in ancient Greece and Rome. One version of a ball-and-stick game from Mesoamerica (now Mexico and Central America) was played with a puck that was set on fire.

An indigenous group of people from Chile are shown here playing one of the games that inspired the creation of hockey.

Some historians think that hockey-like games were also played in North Africa, India, Korea, and Japan.

In 1997, builders made an exciting sculpture discovery as they excavated for a golf course. According to journalist Alisha Jeter, "The piece depicts five life-size Cheyenne Indians engaged in the ancient game of shinny in which a ball is hit on a field."[3]

Many of these ball-and-stick games evolved into modern games such as golf, lacrosse, field hockey, and ice hockey. In some countries, the older forms are being revived as part of an effort to honor each country's roots.

Ball-and-Stick Games

Archaeological findings suggest that groups of native people in the northern areas of the world were playing a ball-and-stick game on the ice many centuries ago. These games were played using bent sticks and a painted wooden ball. The object was to hit the ball through the opposing team's goal. Ten men played on each team. The Micmac group of eastern Canada, for instance, called their game *tooadijik*, while indigenous people in other lands used different names.

The English and Russians played a similar game called bandy as early as the 10th and 11th centuries. This game originated as a form of field hockey played on ice. It was especially popular in Russia because of the long winters there. Bandy was played using a stick and ball. Two teams of 8 to 11 players competed to get the ball into the other team's goal. Today, bandy is still a popular sport, and it is played in the United States, Canada, Sweden, Norway, and other countries with cold, icy winters.

The origins of a game called hurling, which was played in Great Britain, Ireland, and Scotland, dates back to the seventh century. It was played in the winter, when the fields were frozen. Players used a square wooden block that was hit with a stick. Players strapped blades made of wood or bone onto their shoes to help propel them across the freezing tundra. By the 17th century, almost every European country with a cold climate played some form of the game.

By the middle of the 19th century, the Dutch developed a primitive but more practical form of ice skates by strapping metal blades onto their shoes. The blades allowed the skaters to perform with more balance and speed. They gave the players better traction on the ice, and the blades were also less likely to become loose and cause players to fall. Ice hockey increased in popularity as a result of the new skates.

The word "hockey," however, did not come into existence until the end of the 19th century. One theory historians have on the origin of the term is it comes from the French word *hoquet*, a word describing the shape of a shepherd's crook, since a hockey stick resembles the crook. Additionally, the first record of the rules of the game comes from Colonel Byron Weston, who was stationed in Nova Scotia, Canada. In an interview with well-known sports reporter James Power, he related the rules of the game, which came to be called the Halifax Rules.

Power Play

The first puck used during an outdoor game of hockey was made out of frozen cow dung. Other early pucks were made from wood.

Canada's Official Winter Sport

Whatever the origin of the name, ice hockey was brought to Canada from Great Britain and other European countries during the 1800s. Hockey soon became the country's official national winter sport. While the Canadians did not invent the game of hockey, they are credited with refining it into the game that is played today.

Historical records indicate that the first semiofficial game occurred in Kingston, Ontario, in the 1850s between Canadian soldiers stationed there. Three different Canadian cities later claimed the credit for introducing ice hockey to North America: Halifax, Nova Scotia; Kingston, Ontario; and Montreal, Québec. The first officially sanctioned indoor hockey game played with a flat circular piece of wood, complete with written rules and regulations, was played in 1875 between two McGill University teams at the Victoria Skating Rink in Montreal. According to Gary Abraham, a sports medicine specialist in youth hockey, "it was organized by James Creighton, a Halifax engineer whom many call the father of organized ice hockey."[4] Creighton was part of the Ottawa hockey club called the Rideau Hall Rebels.

In the 1880s, a square piece of rubber called a puck replaced the ball or block of wood that had been used for centuries. The Victoria Hockey Club of Montreal is credited with using the first rubber hockey pucks.

In 1890, the Ontario Hockey Association was formed; it was the first organization created to administer the increasingly popular game of ice hockey. During the late 19th century, many Canadian towns and cities had hockey teams. These teams played in unorganized leagues, and their games were fiercely competitive. Many cities had more than one team. The players on these teams were not paid by anyone to play.

Many of the rules used in these early games became the basis for the rules that are used today in modern hockey. However, the game that was played in the late 19th century barely resembles the modern one. There were nine players on each team, and players did not wear any protective equipment. In addition, players were not allowed to make any forward passes. Spectators stood on the edge of the ice with no protection from flying pucks.

One thing that has not changed, however, is the size of hockey ice rinks. Rink dimensions were first established by the ice surface at Montreal's Victoria Skating Rink, which was 200 feet (61 m) by 85 feet (26 m).

Power Play

The number of people who attended a game between the Michigan State University Spartans and the University of Michigan Wolverines on December 11, 2010— 104,173 people— was the largest crowd to ever attend a college hockey game.

Ice Hockey Arrives in the United States

Ice hockey first appeared in the United States in the late 19th century. Initially, only those living in the Northeast and Upper Midwest, where the climate was amenable to the creation of frozen ponds and lakes, were interested in the game. As late as 1895, many American teams were still using a ball instead of a puck because of the availability of balls and the higher cost of pucks. More formal hockey games began with a game between teams from Yale University and Johns Hopkins University in 1896.

While still largely a game played by amateurs and college students, hockey took a more professional turn in 1904, when the first professional hockey league—the International Professional Hockey League (IPHL)—was formed in Houghton, Michigan. Teams from both the United States and Canada belonged to the league. After the 1906 and 1907 season, the league ended. Many teams disbanded as players wanted to play closer to home and in front of home crowds. There were also more professional opportunities in Canada, which drew back players from the IPHL. These professional Canadian teams, located mainly in Ontario and Quebec, formed the National Hockey Association, which ran from 1910 to 1917.

In 1917, the National Hockey Association dissolved as some team executives left to form the National Hockey League (NHL). Initially, only Canadian teams belonged to this professional league, and they played against the Pacific Coast Hockey Association for the championship title. In 1924, however, the Boston Bruins of Massachusetts were invited to join, and other U.S. teams soon followed. The league then expanded quickly, and after 1926, the championship was determined within the league.

Professional Hockey Begins

Professional ice hockey started slowly and gradually attracting more interest and money. During the early years of the NHL, the game was quite different than it is today. In the beginning, players could not pass the puck forward, goalies could not drop to the ice and smother the puck, and the rules were constantly changing.

Hockey historian Douglas Hunter explained, "[Hockey's] most fundamental rules were revised ceaselessly, even decades into its existence as a popular professional sport. Baseball as played in the 1920s was much the same as it is today, but a hockey fan transported back into a rinkside seat before the Depression [in the 1930s] would find the game [of hockey] decidedly odd."[5] Gradually, however, many of the rules changed, play became standardized, and the more modern game of hockey emerged.

Ice Hockey as an Olympic Sport

Hockey teams from many countries around the world compete every four years in the Olympic Games. Men's ice hockey became an Olympic event in 1920. (Women's ice hockey first appeared at the 1998 Olympics.) Seven teams entered that first competition: Canada, the United States, Switzerland, Belgium, France, Sweden, and Czechoslovakia. Canada won in 1920 and in five of the next six competitions, while the Russian team dominated the competition in the 1960s and 1970s.

One of the most startling victories in Olympic ice hockey history came in 1980, when a team of amateur players from the United States captured the gold medal in a stunning upset of the heavily favored Russian and Finnish teams. Called the "Miracle on Ice," the game between the United States and the Soviet Union heightened interest in hockey in the United States. Sports historians consider the U.S. victory one of the greatest upsets in sports history.

For 77 years, only amateurs could compete in Olympic ice hockey. Starting in 1998, NHL players (professional athletes) were allowed to participate in the Olympics.

The U.S. Olympic ice hockey team won the "Miracle on Ice" game against the Soviet Union on February 22, 1980, in Lake Placid, New York.

Today's NATIONAL HOCKEY LEAGUE

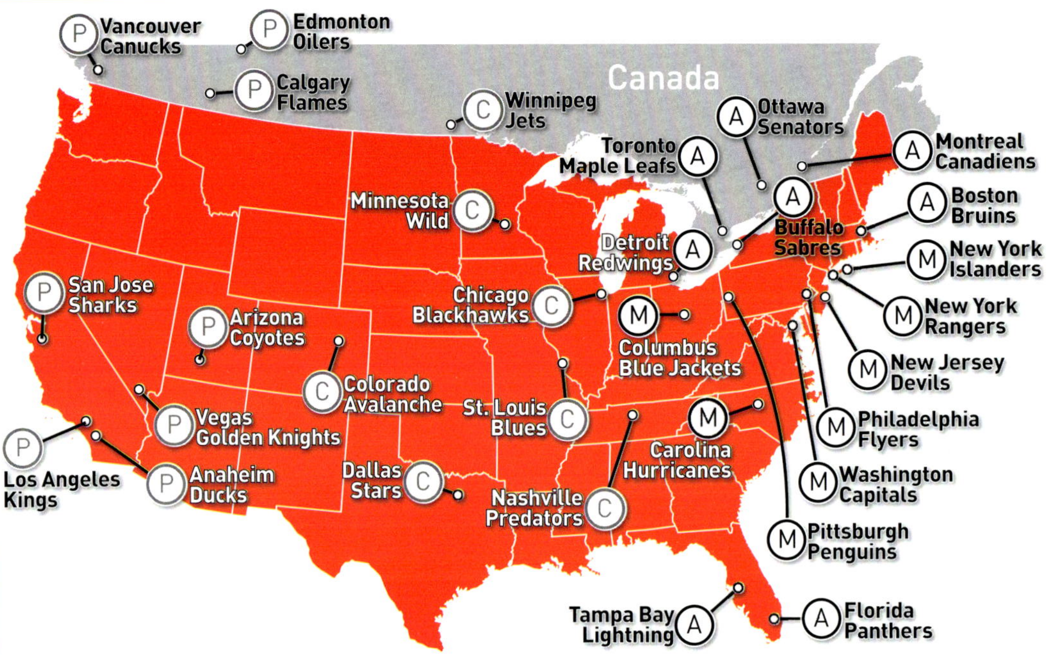

Western Conference
- (P) Pacific
- (C) Central

Eastern Conference
- (A) Atlantic
- (M) Metropolitan

Today, the NHL is made up of 31 teams; 24 are in the United States, and 7 are in Canada.

Hockey's golden age began in 1942 and lasted for 25 years. During that time, the NHL had only six teams: the Boston Bruins, the Chicago Blackhawks, the New York Rangers, the Detroit Red Wings, the Montreal Canadiens, and the Toronto Maple Leafs. This period was "golden" because of the immense popularity of the game and the fierce rivalry that existed between the "Original Six" teams.

It was during this time that the season was expanded to 70 games. The season used to have 24 games during the early part of the 20th century and 48 games prior to World War II.

The composition of professional hockey teams also changed during this period. In the early years of professional hockey, the teams were made up of only Canadian and American players. That changed by the 1990s, when players from all over the world were recruited to play in North America. The fall of the Berlin Wall and the collapse of the former Soviet Union made it possible for players from Communist countries to play for the first time in North America. The first to be given permission to play in the NHL was Sergei Priakin from Russia in 1989. He was soon joined by hundreds of players from Russia, Czechoslovakia, Sweden, Finland, and elsewhere.

As of 2017, the NHL is made up of 31 teams. Six teams were added to the original six in 1967, with additional expansions in 1970 and every two years after that. In 1979, four teams were added to the NHL, and there was not another expansion until 1991 with the addition of the San Jose Sharks. More teams were added in 1992, 1993, 1998, 1999, and 2000, with the total number of teams reaching 30. The Vegas Golden Knights joined in the 2017–2018 season, bringing the total to 31 teams. There are two conferences, the Eastern Conference and the Western Conference. There are two divisions in the Eastern Conference, the Atlantic Division and Metropolitan Division, and each division has eight teams. In the Western Conference, the Central Division has seven teams, and the Pacific Division has eight teams. This team organization started in the 2013–2014 season. During the playoffs, eight teams from each conference play in three rounds that are each a best of seven series. The top team from each conference then faces each other in a best of seven series to determine the winner. The Stanley Cup has been awarded to ice hockey's best team since the late 19th century.

Ice hockey has also become a popular sport on television, especially in Canada. On February 25, 1940, the first hockey game was shown on television: the New York Rangers versus the Montreal Canadiens. In 1952, the Canadian Broadcasting Company (CBC) began transmitting television signals in Canada. The first televised game in Canada was broadcast on October 11, 1952, from Toronto, allowing avid hockey fans in Canada to watch their favorite sport without being at the arena. In 2007, the CBC and the NHL formed a partnership to show the games through 2014. Viewership often reached the 3 million mark. In 2013, the NHL and Rogers Communications formed a new partnership to show the games through the 2025–2026 season.

Outdoor Roots

Professional ice hockey returned to its outdoor roots for the 2008 NHL Winter Classic, when the Pittsburgh Penguins defeated the Buffalo Sabres 2–1 on an ice-covered field at what is now New Era Field, the home of the Buffalo Bills football team. More than 71,000 fans endured the freezing cold to see the game in person. This record was broken during the 2014 NHL Winter Classic when 105,491 fans watched the Toronto Maple Leafs win against the Detroit Red Wings 3–2 at Michigan Stadium in Ann Arbor, Michigan.

From Old Rules to Modern Rules

Since the inception of the game of ice hockey, there have been many changes. In the early years, each hockey team was made up of nine players on the ice, and today's game features only six players—a goalie, two defensemen, two wings, and a center. These players, with the exception of the goalie, are replaced throughout the game in a continuous process, allowing no one player to average more than a minute or so of ice time at any given point. Each team is allotted 18 skaters and 2 goalies. Some players will average more ice time per game than others, depending on their level of skill.

A face-off is used to begin each hockey game. A player from each team faces each other at center ice; the referee then drops the puck, and the play begins by the team who gains possession of the puck. The professional game is divided into 3, 20-minute periods, with an intermission of 18 minutes between each period. In a regular-season game that ends in a tie, the victor is determined during a five-minute sudden-death overtime. This means that the first team that scores wins. If no winner is determined in overtime, the teams go through a process called a shootout. During a shootout, three players from each team try one at a time to shoot a puck into the goal, guarded by the goalie. The team that scores the most times wins the game. If no winner is determined after the original three players, the shootout continues with a sudden death format.

Standings in the NHL are based on a point system in addition to wins and losses. Each team earns two points for an outright win in regulation time (60 minutes), and if the game goes into overtime, the losing team receives one point. At the end of the season, the 16 teams with the highest scores (four from each division) participate in a series of playoff games to determine the best team in the NHL.

Derick Brassard (#19) of the Ottawa Senators and David Backes (#42) of the Boston Bruins are shown here during a face-off in the 2017 NHL Stanley Cup Playoffs.

Modern ice hockey also makes use of a series of penalties that can send the offending player off the ice, typically to a penalty box. The offending player's team is then required to play one player short for the duration of the penalty, which allows the other team an opportunity to score with a man advantage; this is called a power play. Most penalties are categorized as "minor" penalties and last two minutes. Minor penalties are called for tripping, roughing (fighting) that does not cause bleeding, high-sticking (touching the opponent's upper body with the stick) that does not cause bleeding, holding, interference, hooking (using the stick to slow an opponent), delay of game, and too many men on the ice.

Major penalties of five minutes are given for more serious offenses. These involve injury to another player as well as fighting. In some instances, if a serious infraction or injury occurs, the offending player is given a game misconduct penalty and is ejected from the game. Depending on the league, two to four officials are responsible for calling penalties and for enforcing the rules. Four officials (two referees and two linesmen) are used in most professional hockey games.

Power Play

Ice hockey is one of the only sports where one player can be sent into the game to replace another player without a stoppage in play.

Women on the Ice

Hockey is not just a game for men; it is also played by an ever-increasing number of women. From 2000 to 2010, ice hockey became one of the fastest growing women's sports in the world and continued to grow throughout the next decade.

While there is not evidence that governor general Lord Frederick Stanley of Canada played hockey, his family members were enthusiastic spectators of the sport, and his sons and daughter actively played hockey. They begged for a hockey rink at the house where they could play, and their winter parties often involved playing hockey on this rink. This was unusual for both upper-class people and for women at a time when it would be considered unladylike. One of Frederick Stanley's sons, Arthur, helped form the Ontario Hockey Association, and his daughter Isobel Stanley was a pioneer in the sport as one of the first known women to play hockey. Additionally, Isobel and her siblings are responsible for convincing their father to donate a silver cup to be given to a winning team each year: the Stanley Cup.

From Swimming to Sleds

There are many forms of hockey played today. Underwater hockey, for instance, is played in a swimming pool. The puck has a lead core interior weighing 3 pounds (1.4 kg). The added weight makes the puck heavy enough to sink in water but light enough that it can be passed. It is covered with a Teflon, plastic, or rubber coating and painted bright orange or pink. Sticks are made of wood or thick plastic and measure about 12 inches (30 cm) long.

Sledge, or sled hockey, was created in Stockholm, Sweden in the early 1960s for athletes with severe lower body injuries. Players sit in special sleds and play on a standard-size rink with six players. The sleds have skate blades for easy movement, while players use two sticks with ice picks on the bottom to push themselves around the rink and handle the puck. Competitors play in leagues and also in the Winter Paralympic Games, an Olympic event that features several hundred physically impaired athletes competing in a

1. Quoted in "Sled Hockey," Disabled Sports USA, accessed May 12, 2017. www.disabledsportsusa.org/sport/sled-hockey/.

variety of sports. Tom Carr is the assistant director of outreach and athletics at Northeast Passage and a member of the Disabled Sports USA group. He said, "There have been such huge advances in player skill and advances in equipment that the game of sled hockey from the 1990s and the game today is totally unrecognizable ... As a team sport, it's one of the fastest growing."[1]

Underwater hockey is popular in Australia.

Women's hockey teams in Canada and the United States began competing for the first time in 1916. Despite the number of women playing, the game remained largely unknown to the general public. *New York Times* reporter Andrea Kannapell wrote, "For most of [the 20th] century, [women's hockey] was in retreat, hiding out at prep schools and Ivy League colleges."[6] Many girls and women who wanted to play hockey, in fact, were forced to play on boys' and men's teams.

Women eventually wanted more control over the hockey leagues in which they played, and in 1922, they formed the Ladies Ontario Hockey Association. For the first time, women players were able to make decisions about their own game.

The major difference in the men's and women's game is that no body checking (stopping an opponent through the use of physical contact) is allowed in women's hockey. Girls are no longer forced to play on boys' teams; in fact, today, girls are discouraged from playing boys' hockey. This is due to the physical difference between the two sexes. Girls develop differently than boys. Before puberty, boys and girls often compete on the same teams, but as they grow, their

The Buffalo Snow Birds played in the Buffalo, New York, winter wearing bathing suits.

bodies begin to perform differently, leading to the call for different teams.

Interest in women's hockey increased in the late 20th century, especially after the game was added to the 1998 Olympic Games. Gary Abraham explained, "A lot of the increased growth in girls' hockey is due to the Women's World Championship, first held in 1990. But the greatest boost was the 1998 Winter Olympic Games in Nagano, Japan, where women's hockey finally became an Olympic medal sport."[7] The United States won the gold medal at that first Olympic event. At the 2014 games in Sochi, Russia, the gold medal was won by Canada, and the United States won the silver medal.

The number of females playing ice hockey has skyrocketed. In 1990, there were 11,341 female players in Canada and 10,000 in the United States. By 2012, more than 85,500 Canadian women played the sport, along with more than 65,500 in the United States.

In 2015, the National Women's Hockey League (NWHL) was formed with four teams: the Buffalo Beauts, Boston Pride, New York Riveters, and Connecticut Whale. In 2016, the NWHL was given its own trophy cup—the Isobel Cup, named after Isobel Stanley.

The U.S. women's hockey team won the silver medal at the 2014 Winter Olympics.

Women's Accomplishments

Much of the increased popularity in women's hockey is due to the accomplishments of several girls and women. In 1956, nine-year-old Abby Hoffman signed up as "Ab Hoffman" for a local boys' hockey league. Her teammates did not know she was female; dressed in the typical hockey gear, she looked like all the other players. Ab Hoffman was nominated for the All-Star Team and was named one of the best defensemen in the league. However, with being nominated for the All-Star Team, her team manager had to confirm her age by reexamining her birth certificate. When he reexamined it, he discovered that Ab Hoffman was actually a girl. The discovery spread quickly, and her photograph and story appeared in papers throughout North America. She was allowed to continue playing on the boys' team until the end of the season, and then a rule was passed that prohibited girls from playing in boys' leagues. Hoffman is credited with the creation of many girls' leagues throughout North America. Today, the Abby Hoffman Cup is given to the national champion of Canadian women's hockey.

In 1992, Manon Rhéaume became the first woman to sign an NHL contract. She played goalie in one exhibition game with the Tampa Bay Lightning against the St. Louis Blues. After her brief appearance for the Lightning, Rhéaume played in an East Coast Hockey League game and became the first woman to play in an American Hockey League game. She also played on Canada's team in the first women's hockey tournament in the Olympics; the team won the silver medal in 1998.

Angela Ruggiero became the first female non-goalie to play on a men's professional hockey team when she played for the Tulsa Oilers in 2005. Other women to play in men's professional hockey leagues include Erin Whitten, Kelly Dyer, Hayley Wickenheiser, and Kira Hurley. Hurley was the first female goalie to score a point (a goal or an assist) in a men's professional game.

One of the greatest women's hockey teams in history was the Preston Rivulettes of Canada, formed by sisters Hilda and Nellie Ranscombe in 1930. With Hilda playing right wing and Nellie playing goalie, the team amassed an amazing record of 348 wins and only 2 losses. From 1930 to 1939, the team won 10 championship titles in Québec and Ontario, as well as 6 national titles.

Hockey for Younger Players

The popularity of men's and women's hockey has resulted in an ever-increasing interest in youth hockey. According to Abraham, "well over a million kids play hockey in North America. The game has become a large part of our culture."[8]

ICE HOCKEY *by the* NUMBERS

	country	players		country	players
1	Canada	639,500	7	Switzerland	26,898
2	United States	543,239	8	Germany	25,430
3	Czech Republic	109,103	9	France	21,451
4	Russia	102,179	10	Japan	18,988
5	Finland	74,150	11	Great Britain	12,462
6	Sweden	60,408	12	Slovakia	12,380

This chart, based on a 2016 survey by the International Ice Hockey Federation (IIHF), shows the number of hockey players on registered professional and amateur teams in the top 12 listed countries.

In general, most children begin playing ice hockey around the age of five. As the players age, they are moved up to more advanced teams and compete with other teams in the same age group.

Most children wear so much protective gear that their weight is nearly doubled. Unlike in the professional leagues, all players are required to wear helmets and face guards similar to the mask worn by goalies. Coaches run highly structured practices, stressing the importance of skills and proper conditioning. The youth leagues all come under the watchful eye of youth hockey organizations in Canada, the United States, and other countries.

One of today's young heroes is Emma Nichols, who, at age 11, played goalie on a boys' team at a youth tournament in England in 2015. She stopped 35 shots and brought a 3–0 victory to her team, and videos of her playing went viral on social media. Nichols also played on the 2017 England Under 13 team.

Today, thousands of young hockey players from 10 different countries gather once a year to play in the International Ice Hockey Federation (IIHF) World Under-20 Championship (also known as the World Junior Championship). The games alternate host countries each year. The tournament is a 10-day event in which young players under 20 compete. It has become a popular event to watch for hockey fans around the world who want to see the future stars of the sport in action.

An Enduring Prize

Lord Frederick Stanley, governor general of Canada in the late 19th century, lent his name to one of the most enduring prizes in sports history. In 1893, he presented an award to the champion of the Amateur Hockey Association of Canada. That first Stanley Cup, the oldest trophy in professional sports, was awarded to the Montreal Amateur Athletic Association. At that time, the award was called the Dominion Hockey Challenge Cup.

In the early days of competition for the Stanley Cup, any team from any town could compete for the cup. As the game became more professionally oriented, bigger towns became more prominent because of the high cost of paying the best hockey players. When the NHL was created, the trophy was given to the winning team, beginning in 1947. Since that time, the Stanley Cup has been awarded each year as a symbol of hockey supremacy.

The original Stanley Cup, which was made of silver, was 7.28 inches (18.5 cm) high and 11.42 inches (29 cm) in diameter. The modern version, made out of silver and nickel alloy, first appeared in 1958 in a five-band barrel shape that weighs 34.5 pounds (15.6 kg) and stands 35.25 inches (89.54 cm) high.

Since 1993, each member of the winning team gets one day in the summer to keep the cup. They often show it to fans and supporters. When Pittsburgh Penguins coach Mike Sullivan had the cup, he said, "We wanted to share it with as many people as we can that have had an influence in our life, but also the next generation coming up ... I think [the Stanley Cup] is a great inspiration. ... It's amazing how many people it has an influence and an impact on."[1]

1. Quoted in Shawn P. Roarke, "Stanley Cup has an incredible history," NHL.com, March 13, 2017. www.nhl.com/news/stanley-cup-has-incredible-125-years-of-history/c-287633638.

The Stanley Cup is given to the winner of the NHL Championship every year.

Players can get further experience in junior leagues, as well as in colleges in Canada and the United States. Competition is fierce throughout the collegiate ranks, especially in the United States. American teams play a season-ending tournament called the Frozen Four that attracts many fans each year.

Ice hockey continues to grow in popularity at all levels of competition. As a result of the increased popularity of the sport, many teams sell out their season tickets each year, and television audiences tune in to watch NHL games. Today, ice hockey remains an exciting and action-packed game at all levels of play.

The U.S. team is shown here celebrating after their win at the 2017 IIHF World Junior Championships.

Chapter 2

The Physics of Hockey

Watching a hockey game is an exciting, tense experience. Anxious fans watch their favorite team play and hope for a win while booing or cheering at every penalty, every goal, and the overall action on the ice. However, there is a lot more to hockey than what meets the eye.

A fan might not realize that there is a lot of science, specifically physics, behind a game of ice hockey. Without understanding how to apply the scientific concepts of speed, velocity, friction, momentum, motion, energy, and force, ice hockey would not be the game it is today.

Artificial Ice

Ice surfaces have improved dramatically since the early days of hockey, when players used snow-covered, bumpy frozen ponds or other bodies of water. Because of the need for a surface of ice, hockey could only be played during the coldest winter months and mostly outdoors.

The first indoor hockey game was played in Montreal in 1875. By the early 1900s, covered ice surfaces or arenas were popping up all over North America. The technology used to make and maintain the indoor ice, however, was expensive. Most games, therefore, were still played on natural outdoor ice until the 1940s and 1950s, when a less costly method of freezing the surface was developed.

Today's game is mainly played on specially made ice rinks in large indoor arenas. Before the first hockey game of the season, ice makers throughout the NHL are busy at work preparing their arena's ice surface. Most arenas have an advanced refrigeration system that is capable of pumping large amounts of salt water through a system of pipes onto a large piece of concrete, known as the ice slab. Salt water, or brine water, which is a calcium chloride solution, is used to cool the slab because it has a low freezing temperature and will keep circulating to keep the ice slab at a steady temperature. Fresh water, on the other hand, freezes quicker, and would stop the water from circulating.

Once the slab reaches a cold enough temperature—about 16 degrees Fahrenheit (–8.8 degrees Celsius), layers of water are applied to the slab to build up the proper density and thickness of the ice—generally 0.75 inch (1.9 cm) thick. The proper ice thickness is crucial. Nick Kryshak, official ice technician for the New Jersey Devils, has said of the ice, "It's a living, breathing apparatus … It's not too hard, it's not too chippy, it's not too soft. Every little thing matters. You want that perfect consistency."[9]

The first few layers of the ice surface are typically painted with the team's logo and any advertisements. Regulation markings, such as lines and circles, are also added. Since these markings are integral to the game, the sizes must match league specifications. Technicians do this by using geometry, giant rulers, and string gauges to

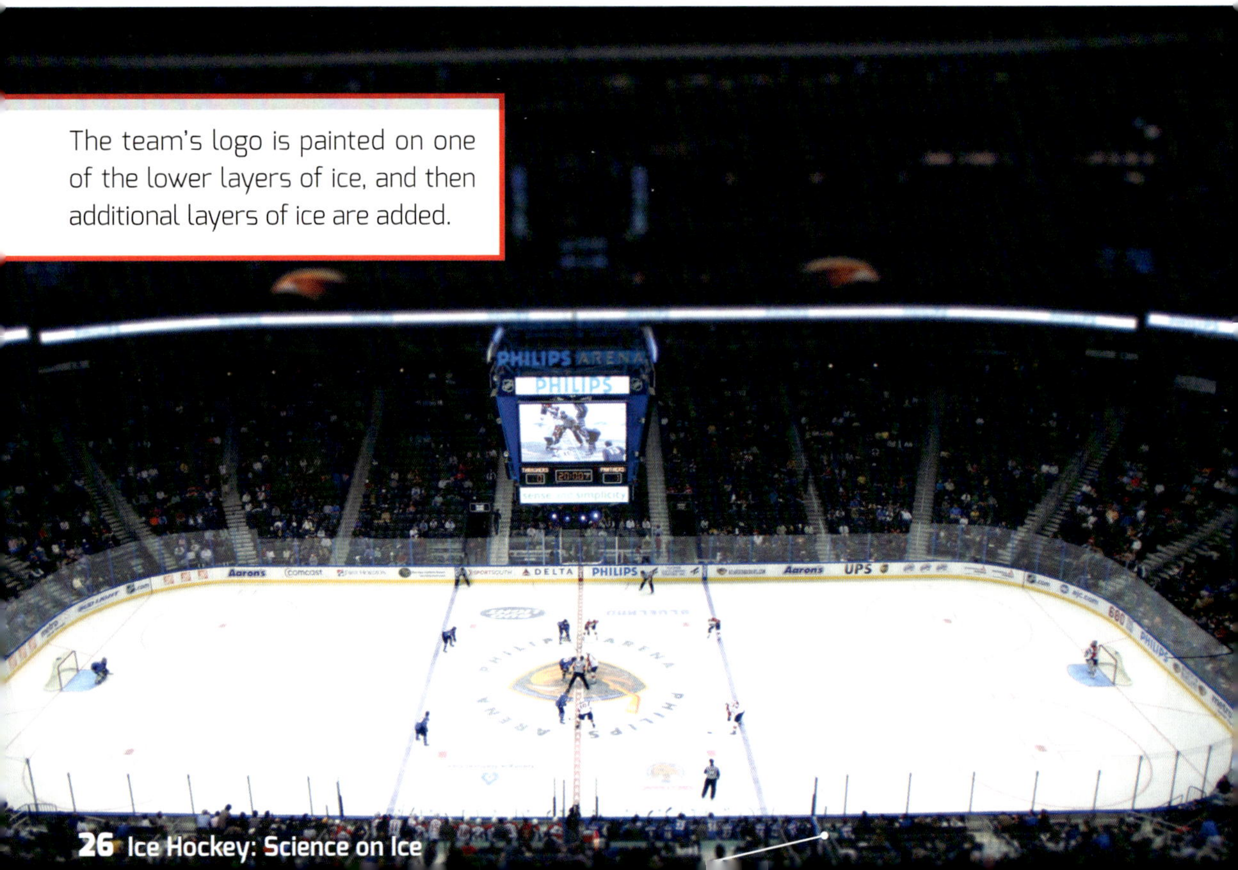

The team's logo is painted on one of the lower layers of ice, and then additional layers of ice are added.

measure the shapes before painting. After the logos and other markings are painted, additional layers of ice are added, bringing the total frozen water used to about 10,600 gallons (40,125 L). The water is applied slowly, generally about 600 gallons (2,271 L) at a time. Applying the water too quickly or in large quantities results in an uneven surface with many irregularities that would endanger the skaters. Many ice supervisors use sonar depth guns to check if the ice is even across the rink. The entire process takes about four days. This ice stays in place from September to May or even longer, if the team does well in the playoffs.

To help keep the ice solid and "fast," the ice is treated after each hockey period. One of the primary tools used to treat the ice is the Zamboni machine, named after its inventor, Frank Zamboni. The Zamboni is a mechanical ice resurfacer that works by washing, shaving, and then collecting the ice shavings. The final step is putting down a thin layer of heated water that melts the top layer of ice. The warm water also melts any small ruts in the ice made from the players' skates. When this warm top layer freezes, it creates a smooth ice surface. The ideal temperature for this water is around 140 degrees Fahrenheit (60 degrees Celsius).

Fast Ice and Slow Ice

The terms "fast ice" and "slow ice" are commonplace in hockey leagues around the world. According to scientists, "fast ice is harder and colder with a smoother surface, while slow ice is warm and soft and may have a rough surface."[10]

Additionally, to keep the ice "fast," it has to stay cold. The ideal temperature for the top of the ice is generally between 24 and 26 degrees Fahrenheit (–4.4 and 3.3 degrees Celsius). Maintaining this temperature is more difficult in milder climates because of the warmer outside air temperature.

The Zamboni is important for maintaining the quality of the ice during the game so players can best demonstrate their skill.

Hockey players know which arenas have the best ice. Canadian hockey rinks, for instance, are well-known for the high quality of their ice because of the climate in the region. To keep the quality of the ice, the arena and ice temperatures need to be adjusted to compensate for the climate and the heat that will come in the arena when the doors are opened and fans arrive. However, even in colder regions such as Canada, there is still a certain amount of work that technicians need to do to maintain the ice quality. Often, the arenas in Canada need to be heated because the low temperatures can create problems with the ice.

The quality of ice impacts how the game is played. This was especially seen during the 2016–2017 season, in which there were complaints on the quality of the ice in numerous hockey rinks and a number of games were postponed or delayed due to the ice. New York Rangers head coach Alain Vigneault said, "I know the ice was the same for both teams, but the quality of the ice today was just horrendous … When you can't put two passes together because the puck is bouncing all over the place, makes it very hard on both players, who have some skill. It makes it hard to put that skill on display."[11] Ryan Miller, a goaltender in the NHL since 2002, called the ice the worst he had played on in his entire career.

Today's Rink

The ice rink itself has not changed much since the inception of the modern game. The dimensions of the hockey rinks that were established in Canada in the 1870s have not changed. The appearance and layout of the rink, however, have changed during the following decades.

Today's ice rink is surrounded by a series of boards that not only keep the puck in play but also offer a backboard for executing a pass or clearing the puck out of the team's zone. The boards range from 40 to 48 inches (101.6 to 122 cm) above the ice surface. In addition, the boards must be white with the exception of authorized advertising and the yellow kickboard that runs the entire length of the boards. On top of the boards, there is a second wall of shatterproof tempered glass or Plexiglas, which is an acrylic plastic sheet. High netting is also used around the scoring ends of the rink to prevent the puck from flying into the stands.

Two blue lines, each 12 inches (30 cm) wide, divide the playing surface into three separate zones. These are called the defending, attacking, and neutral zones. The distance between the end of the rink and a blue line is 75 feet (22 m), with 64 feet (19.5 m) between the blue line and the goal line.

Between each of the blue lines is the neutral zone, which is 50 feet (15 m) wide. Additionally, a center red line that is 12 inches (30 cm) wide divides the rink into 2 equal halves.

At each end of the hockey rink, there is a metal frame holding a cloth net, which serves as the goal. The dimensions of the net itself are 6 feet by 4 feet (1.8 m by 1.2 m). In front of the net is the goal crease, which is the area where the goaltender stays during games to defend the net from opposing players. This area with a 6-foot (1.8 m) radius, which is outlined by thin red lines, is painted light blue. Invasion of the goal crease by an opposing player is called interference and results in a penalty.

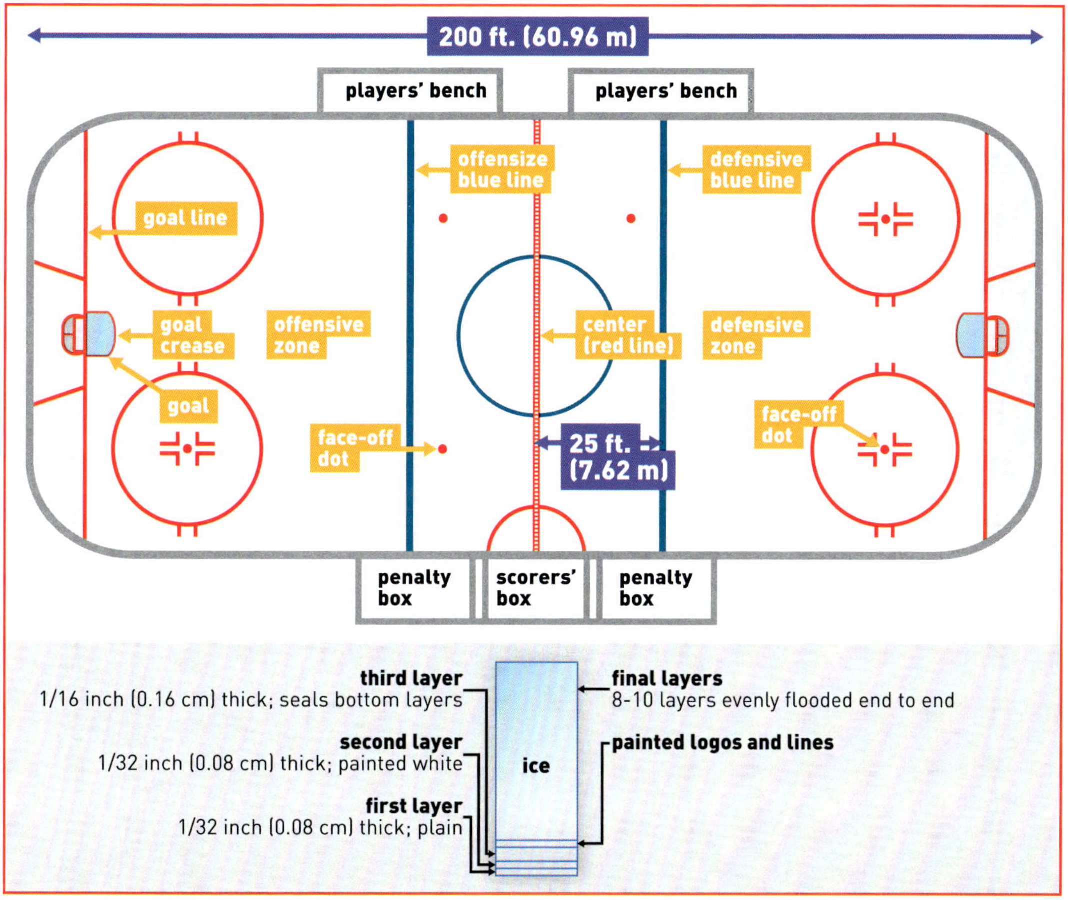

The markings on a hockey rink are regulated by the NHL, and each rink must match league specifications.

Power Play

In 1914, a rule was passed that allowed hockey officials to drop the puck between the players' sticks for face-offs. Prior to 1914, the officials placed the puck on the ice and often ended up with bruises, cuts, and broken bones

Exciting Discoveries

Chemist Gabor Somorjai discovered that a person actually skates on vibrating molecules. Journalist Kirsten Weir explained, "Like all matter, ice is composed of particles called molecules. At the surface of the ice, the molecules exist in a part-solid, part-liquid state. That quasi-liquid layer makes ice slick."[12]

For years, scientists believed that friction (the force that exists when one object rubs against another) and pressure caused the ice to melt, thus providing a slicker surface, which enabled skaters to glide more efficiently. Somorjai discovered that skates and pucks did not create enough pressure to cause melting. Instead, the quasi-liquid layer of ice created by the vibrating molecules was sufficient to keep the ice slick.

This layer of quasi-liquid ice is thin. A warmer ice rink, however, adds depth to this layer and creates slower ice. With additional layers, the ice becomes slushy; creating more friction that slows down the players. This is one reason why ice rinks are kept so cold. At warmer temperatures, too much melting occurs.

Gliding Across the Ice

Putting pressure on ice by standing or skating across it melts a thin layer of ice. As the ice melts and creates water, the ice surface becomes slippery. When combined with the pressure or rubbing of a skate against the ice, the friction between the ice and the skate is greatly reduced. This allows the skater to easily glide across the ice. Weir explained, "Very little friction exists between ice and skates."[13] Friction is the force resisting motion on solid surfaces. The larger the object moving along a solid surface,

Figure Skates Vs. Hockey Skates

Ice hockey skates are different than figure skating skates. While both skates have a hollow area between two sharp edges, in figure skating, the skater uses only one edge at a time, which creates a smoother glide on the ice. Hockey players use both edges, and the boot is sturdier and higher to protect the feet. In addition, figure skaters have a large set of jagged teeth on the front of the blade, called a toe pick. These are used in jumping and intricate footwork.

the greater the friction and the less quickly that object moves. According to experts, "the friction between the [skate] blade and the ice is minimized because the surface of the ice is so slippery, and because only a small portion of the skate's blade is actually in contact."[14]

Early Skates

The first ice skates were created around 3000 BC and were made of animal bones. The bones were tied to the bottoms of shoes with some form of rope but were unreliable because the rope would often loosen, causing the bones to fall off. To correct this problem, the Dutch created wooden skates in the 14th century; these were slightly more effective and less prone to falling off. The wood, however, did not always glide well across the ice, and the wood absorbed moisture and made the skates heavy.

Eventually, iron blades replaced bone and wooden blades. Iron blades were thinner and sharper, leaving a smaller surface actually in contact with the ice, which created less friction between the blades and the ice. They also did not absorb water from the ice like bone and wooden blades did. An ice skater screwed this skate onto the sole of their boot. Because the screws sometimes came loose, straps made of leather or rope were also used to hold the skates securely to the foot.

The Dutch made wooden skates such as these in the 14th century.

19th, 20th, and 21st Century Skates

Despite the reduced friction that allowed easier gliding, the old skates with straps and screws would often loosen and come off while the individual was moving. This severely limited the kind of skating people could do.

In 1863, after numerous complaints about the durability of skates, John Forbes of Starr Manufacturing Company, along with his assistant, Thomas Bateman, began to work on improving the skates. What players wanted was an all-metal, self-fastening skate. Forbes and Bateman came up with the Starr Acme Skate, a skate that did not require leather strapping. Instead, the Acme Skate clamped onto a boot with a lever that was adjustable to any foot size. Because of its affordability and durability, the Starr Acme Skate was soon selling throughout North America. Many historians credit this scientific invention with changing the face of ice hockey and increasing its popularity in the late 19th century. Finally the skating world had a skate with a blade that would not detach from the boot, improving the quality of skating.

Ice hockey skates evolved throughout the 19th century.

Starr Manufacturing closed in 1939, but by that time, the company had produced more than 19 million pairs of skates. A lighter pair of skates called tube skates was introduced in 1900. This skate was made of steel and was screwed directly onto a skating boot. The skating boot was designed with extra support for the ankle to prevent the ankle from twisting, turning, and being injured during the game. Today's hockey skates have steel blades and a rigid boot that helps protect the player's ankles and feet.

A goaltender's skates are slightly different. The lower half of the goalie skate is covered with a hard plastic shell that protects the goalie's foot from the shock of impact and holds the runner, or the blade. The blade is also cut flatter and has less of a curve because the way the goalie moves is different from the other players. In addition, the boot of the skate is cut shorter to accommodate for the goalie's movements during the game.

A goaltender's skate is created differently to accommodate for quick movement and weight shifts from side to side.

Generating Speed

Proper skates and the slippery surface of the ice allow players to generate speed while skating. The sharp edge of the skate digs into the ice, creating traction, or pulling power; this allows the player to accelerate quickly. Because ice is slippery, the digging in of the skate provides a solid contact with the ice, thus preventing the skates from slipping and providing the player with a quick start. It also allows the player to stop quickly. To stop, most hockey players scrape the ice with the edges of their skates; this creates friction, which helps in slowing down the player.

Professional ice hockey players have been known to reach speeds up to 25 miles (40 km) per hour on the ice. Some players are faster than others, depending on their strength and efficiency on the ice.

According to physicist Thomas Humphrey, skating is "the fastest way to travel on the surface of the earth on your feet."[15] When running, a person is slowed down by his or her feet touching the ground; this creates a large amount of friction between the runner's shoes and the ground. In skating, because there is little friction between the blade and the ice, players can glide across the ice and build up speed as they skate. Speed is the measure of the rate of distance traveled over time. Several speed skaters have been clocked at

Today's Blades

Today skate blades are made of steel. While the blades may look flat, they are actually curved and hollow. Team equipment managers use a process called hollow grinding that produces two sharp edges on the skate with a hollowed-out area in the center. According to experts, "The deeper the hollow, the more 'bite' or grip you'll have on the ice. The more shallow the hollow, the less 'bite' or grip you'll have."[1] In addition,

> *deep hollows will give you great bite on the ice allowing you to turn tighter and more aggressively. As a result, your speed will be reduced as more of the blade will need to dig into the ice to give you this agility and tight turns. On the other hand, a shallow hollow will keep a bigger portion of the blade on the surface of the ice allowing you to go faster and with less effort.*[2]

1. "Ice Hockey Skate Blade Profiling and Skate Sharpening—Hard Ice vs Soft Ice (Fast Ice vs Slow Ice)," Hockey Tutorial, March 31, 2013. www.hockeytutorial.com/ice-hockey-tips/ice-hockey-skate-blade-profiling-skate-sharpening-hard-ice-soft-ice-fast-ice-slow-ice/.

2. "Ice Hockey Skate Blade Profiling and Skate Sharpening—Hard Ice vs Soft Ice (Fast Ice vs Slow Ice)," Hockey Tutorial.

The depth of the hollow is also dependent on the size of the player and their preference. Each hockey player has their own preference about sharpness and the amount of hollow they want on their skates. For example, goalies often choose a deeper hollow.

The equipment manager is responsible for sharpening and maintaining the team's skates. They use a blade sharpener that has a rotating stone wheel that is capable of creating the hollow part of the skate. The skate blade is passed over the stone wheel to smooth and sharpen the blade. A final pass is made using a light coat of oil to give the blade more polish and smoothness.

Sharp skates are necessary to prevent a player from "losing an edge." When a blade becomes dull, players will sometimes have their skates come out from under them, resulting in a fall. Losing an edge can occur because of a skate's contact with dirt or sand off the ice or because of contact with another skate blade during a collision. When this happens, a player often returns to the locker room for a brief period to have their skate blade resharpened.

Modern ice hockey skates are made of steel and hollowed inwardly to give the player more stability.

more than 30 miles (48 km) per hour, with some reaching 37 miles (59 km) per hour. In comparison, speed runners run around 23 miles (37 km) per hour.

According to ice hockey expert and trainer Laura Stamm, speed is affected by a combination of several elements:

> • *Proper skating technique.*
>
> • *Power (pushing correctly and with explosive force).*
>
> • *Leg speed (quickness).*
>
> *A combination of all these elements can yield an explosively fast skater …*
>
> *Every skating maneuver has a two-fold weight shift on every stride—first from pushing skate/leg to gliding skate/leg, and then from gliding skate/leg to pushing skate/leg. The ability to shift weight properly and at the right instant is an extremely important element.*[16]

When players dig their skates into the ice to accelerate, they also lean forward, exerting a strong force on their legs and hips. Gravity then pulls down the player's body mass, which gives them better traction on the ice; this helps propel them forward. In addition, a player's arms and shoulders are important in skating because they help the body maintain balance; they act as a counterbalance to the legs and feet and provide more equilibrium.

Skating on a Curve

A crossover is a maneuver that enables players to accelerate on curves. According to Stamm, a crossover refers to "the passing of the outside skate (the one nearer the outside of the curve) over (in front of) the toe of the inside skate. Additionally, [crossovers] make it possible for players to generate speed for the straight-aways, to weave in and out of traffic, to zigzag down the ice, change direction, turn from backward to forward, and move laterally (from side to side) and to fake."[17] These moves are an essential part of hockey.

A skater must make several quick, precise moves to complete a backwards crossover.

Centripetal force is the scientific principle that enables the player to skate in a circular path. The force is directed toward the center around which the body or object is moving. An example of centripetal force occurs when someone whirls a stone around by a string. The person's hands exert an inner pull or centripetal force on the stone to keep it moving.

In hockey, a player relies on the same inner pull when turning a corner. Stamm explained,

> *Skating on circles and curves … involves powerful forces that tend to oppose the skater's desired directionality … Centripetal force is created by the blades thrusting against the ice (toward the center of the circle) at a strong angle. As the skater's lower body (skates, knees, hips) leans inward … gravitational forces work to make the skater fall. The object of the skater is to keep the curve tight and to minimize wasted distance … while remaining upright and balanced … The entire lower body … leans into [the] circle at a strong angle. To prevent a fall, the upper body … must be situated directly above the center of gravity … located directly above the skates. To balance over the center of gravity, the skater must "counter-lean" with the upper body (lean slightly toward the outside of the circle). By counter-leaning, the upper body will be situated above the center of gravity. The lower body can now safely lean into the circle to skate the circle or curve.*[18]

Thus, the weight shift is from the inside to the outside of the skates, rather than from front to back. This shift in weight helps the skater to remain upright.

In addition to speed and centripetal force, velocity is also a factor in crossovers. Speed measures the rate at which a person or object travels, while velocity also includes direction; it describes change of position. In motion that occurs in a straight line, speed and velocity are the same. On the other hand, when motion occurs along a curve, as it does in crossovers, the velocity is always changing because the direction of the skater is different. This change in velocity can affect balance as players make their quick turns on the ice; thus the player must move their body in the proper way to maintain control.

Some hockey players are able to perform such maneuvers more easily than others. Learning to balance various body parts takes a lot of practice, but can result in much quicker skating and maneuvering.

Motion and Momentum

Ice hockey is a physical sport. Checking, or using physical force to disrupt another player or gain possession of the puck, is what makes hockey a collision sport. The scientific laws of motion and momentum play a significant role in checking and collisions on the ice.

Body checking is allowed in professional hockey, but it is not permitted in youth hockey due to the potential for serious injuries.

Motion is the change of position or location of an object with respect to time. Momentum is a measure of the amount of motion of an object. Science has shown that any free-moving object will travel in a straight line unless some force acts upon it. This is the foundation of the laws of motion, first formulated by Sir Isaac Newton.

Newton was an English physicist, astronomer, and philosopher who developed a number of scientific principles. Considered one of the most influential scientists in history, Newton is best known for his work on understanding gravity and the laws of motion.

There are three laws of motion. The law of inertia states that an object's speed and direction will remain constant unless acted upon by outside influences. When a force of some kind strikes an object, the second law comes into play. This law states that the object will accelerate in the direction of the force and in proportion to the strength of that force. The third law comes into effect during collisions of two objects and states that if a force is applied to an object, the object will react with an opposite and equal force.

To determine momentum, an object's mass is multiplied by its velocity. If the mass of the object is always constant, to change momentum, it is necessary to change the velocity. Thus, an object can be slowed down or sped up by changing its direction. Momentum, therefore, is dependent upon both the velocity and mass of a moving object, as is the force created when two objects collide.

These laws come into play in hockey when players check each other. A body check is when one player intentionally slams into another player, especially one with the puck, so that the other player loses control of the puck or is unable to advance toward the goal.

Although most checking involves knocking an opposing player into the boards, some checking results in collisions between two fast-moving players. Applied force is the force that is shown during this kind of collision; it is a force applied to an object or a person.

The following example illustrates what a collision would be like between two real-life hockey players: Team A's player is moving about 20 miles (32 km) per hour down the ice on his way to shoot the puck. His opponent, Team B's player, is determined to stop him and heads toward Player A while moving 15 miles (24 km) per hour. Player A weighs 200 pounds (91 kg), while Player B weighs 220 pounds (100 kg). A collision between these two players would result in more than 5,800 joules, which is a metric measure of energy. This creates enough energy to light a 60-watt light bulb for 96 seconds.

Each player will experience the same tremendous force in the collision, because, according to Newton's third law, for every action, there is an equal and opposite reaction. At least one player will end up falling on the ice, maybe both. There is also a chance that one or both players will be injured simply because of the intense impact between them. This is why players are taught to check properly to avoid injury.

One type of checking in professional ice hockey is knocking an opponent into the boards.

This kind of collision is legal in hockey. Penalties are called, however, for sending an opposing player into the boards headfirst. This is dangerous because the force of this kind of impact on the head of the opposing player can cause serious injuries and even threaten the career of the injured player.

All hockey collisions can result in injuries. These injuries occur because of the tremendous force that is created by the collision.

Chapter 3

Shooting and Stopping the Puck

According to hockey legend Wayne Gretzky, "A good hockey player plays where the puck is. A great hockey player plays where the puck is going to be."[19]

The advances in sports science over the last few decades have helped players learn how to play where the puck is going to be. When players understand how to use the concepts of friction, gravity, energy, and momentum to shoot and stop the puck, their games improve. The right amount of force applied to a hockey stick can make the puck sail down the ice. A goalie who takes the speed and velocity of the puck and the players into account most likely improves their reaction time.

Changes to Hockey Pucks

The hockey puck has undergone many changes in its history. Native Americans played the game with wooden balls, beaded buckskin balls stuffed with bison fur, or even frozen cow dung.

Early ice hockey players generally used a lacrosse ball, but they soon found that the ball bounced too much on a hard ice surface, making it hard to control and score goals. By 1885, players were cutting off the top and bottom of the lacrosse ball and playing with the flat center piece.

Today, a standard ice hockey puck is black and measures 1 inch (2.5 cm) thick and 3 inches (7.6 cm) in diameter. It weighs about 6 ounces (170 g). Other colors and weights are used at different levels of hockey. For example, the blue 4-ounce (113 g) puck allows young players to develop their technique, while the orange 10-ounce (283 g) puck allows players to improve muscle strength. As far as the thickness is concerned, a thicker and heavier puck would be more dangerous for the players in terms of potential injury, whereas a thinner or lighter one would not be heavy enough to travel with any degree of accuracy.

Many NHL teams use as many as 5,000 pucks a year, and 25 to 30 pucks are used in each game. Pucks are made of vulcanized rubber. Vulcanization is a chemical process that uses high pressure and extreme temperatures to convert rubber into more durable materials. Huge batches of rubber are mixed with chemical agents and coal dust and then put into machines that make a roll of rubber 3 inches (7.6 cm) wide. A slicer cuts the rubber roll into pucks, which are placed in molds. The molds create a dimple pattern along the edge, which creates more friction between the puck and hockey stick, allowing for greater control. Once in the molds, the pucks are cooked at around 365 degrees Fahrenheit (185 degrees Celsius). When they have finished cooking and cooling, they are shipped to a separate facility to have the NHL logo silk-screened on one side and the team logo on the other side. Hockey pucks are made in only a few countries, notably Canada, Russia, the Czech Republic, and China.

Pucks are frozen prior to game use to reduce the potential for bouncing during play and to make them slide better. According to the NHL Officials Association,

> *Game pucks are made of vulcanized rubber and when warm they can be very bouncy! These freezers [that are kept in the penalty boxes] are kept at a temperature between 14F and 20F (-10C to -7C) … Also, in an effort to provide the players with the best possible puck each and every shift, the puck is changed for a new frozen puck every time a puck has been used for more than two minutes of actual playing time. This is done in order to bring consistency to every shift for the players on how the puck will react … In addition to the two minutes of playing time exchanges, the game puck is also changed at every commercial time-out.*[20]

Freezing decreases bouncing by hardening the rubber. Rubber is a soft substance made up of long polymers (large molecules with many structural units) that have elastic properties; they are able to stretch and then return to their previous size and shape. Freezing the rubber reduces the ability of the molecules to stretch, making the puck less prone to bouncing.

While small in size, pucks can be dangerous for a hockey player who gets hit by one. Pucks can reach speeds of more than 100 miles (161 km) per hour when they are struck by a stick on the

Shown here is a worker at a factory in the Czech Republic as he removes hockey pucks from a special oven and sets them out to cool.

ice. Players who get struck by a flying puck can suffer from lacerations, broken bones, eye injuries, lost teeth, and concussions. Spectators are also occasionally injured. The most serious incident took place on March 16, 2002, when a 13-year-old girl died two days after being hit in the head by a flying puck during a Blue Jackets game in Columbus, Ohio.

Partly as a result of this incident, Plexiglas panels that sit atop the boards to protect spectators have been supplemented with large mesh nets that extend higher in the air. In addition, prior to each hockey game, fans are warned by the arena announcer about the possibility of pucks flying into the spectator area. Fans are urged to watch the puck to avoid potential injury. In spite of these precautions, fans still get injured. A fan was hit in the face in 2013, and a puck hit another fan in the head during a 2014 game.

The Law of Action and Reaction

Once a puck is hit, its actions are governed by the scientific law of action-reaction. This means that when there is a collision between two objects (the stick making contact with the puck or the puck making contact with the boards), there is an equal force applied to both objects. The smaller object, in this case the puck, will accelerate.

The following experiment can be done at home to show the difference between a frozen puck and a warmer one:

1. Take two pucks (or two baseballs). Put one in the freezer and leave it there for two to three hours. Leave the other puck or ball at room temperature.

2. Find a cement surface that is relatively flat.

3. While wearing safety equipment such as goggles, drop the pucks or balls from waist level and notice how they bounce.

4. You will immediately notice that the room-temperature puck or ball bounces higher than the frozen one.

5. Throw the pucks or balls up in the air and allow them to bounce. Once again, observe the difference between the two.

Why does the warm puck or ball bounce higher? A warm object is more flexible. Because of this, the energy stored within it is released more quickly and effectively than with the frozen object.

An Essential Tool

A hockey stick is an essential tool for all ice hockey players and is used to shoot, pass, and propel the puck across the ice. The length of a hockey stick is dependent on the player's height, and it is composed of a long shaft with a flat extension at the end, called the blade. The blade is the only part of the stick that comes in contact with the puck.

The blade is attached to the stick at an angle of around 135 degrees, giving the stick an L-shape appearance. This angle is dependent in part on a player's height. Hockey experts explain, "Players usually seek a lie [an angle of the blade] that will put their blade flat on the ice while they are in their typical skating stance."[21] By having the blade flat on the ice, a hockey player has more control of the puck.

The length of the ice hockey stick depends on the player's height.

Power Play

The fastest ice hockey slapshot to date was hit by Denis Kulyash in 2011. It traveled at a speed of 110.3 miles (177.5 km) per hour.

In the early days of ice hockey, most hockey sticks were made of wood. The earliest players often carved their own sticks from a single piece of wood. The first manufactured sticks sold by the Starr Manufacturing Company were sticks carved by the local Mi'kMaq Native American group. The stick was made from the hornbeam tree or yellow birch and was heavy to use and not very flexible.

Next to be used was the two-piece wooden stick, which came into use in the 1920s. The blade was a separate piece that was inserted into the shaft of the stick. In the 1930s and 1940s, the NHL mostly used these two-piece models. In the 1940s, the first laminated sticks appeared. These were made of many layers of wood glued together, which created a lighter, more flexible stick.

During the 1950s, many companies began adding a layer of fiberglass to improve the stick's durability. In the 1960s, the blade of the stick became curved, while in the 1970s, manufacturers continued adopting more synthetic materials, which in turn, created more durable and lighter sticks than before. In the 1980s, aluminum was used for the first time. Aluminum shafts were stiffer than previous models, such as wood or fiberglass, but they offered greater stability. In the 1990s, composite shafts became quite popular because they had the flexibility and stability of wood. Today, the one-piece composite stick is almost universally used, with the exception of some players who choose to stick with the composite shaft and wooden blade.

Scientist Angus McLean said, "Hockey sticks are now designed to flex at certain zones along the shaft."[22] There are actually built-in flex patterns in the stick; rather than stress or energy being focused in one place, it is spread throughout the stick, creating a stronger and more durable piece of equipment.

A duty of an assistant equipment manager is to prepare the sticks for the game.

Although these sticks are a big improvement over earlier sticks, they are also much more expensive to make.

When a player hits the puck, their stick bends forward to create more power; energy is transferred by this action and causes the puck to accelerate. Hockey stick experts explain, "When a player bends his hockey stick when taking a shot, it essentially turns the hockey stick into a spring storing energy. When the spring is released (when the stick unbends and returns to straight), the energy is released and accelerates the puck."[23]

It takes a tremendous force for sticks to break, and in one experiment, "it took nearly one ton of force to break … [the] hockey stick."[24] Despite the improvements, however, hockey sticks do break on occasion. The part of the hockey stick that is most likely to break is the shaft due to repeated impact on the hockey stick. While the shaft is most likely to break, the blade of the stick can also experience damage from the repeated stress it takes during the game from slap shots or even just maneuvering the puck. For this reason, most hockey players have several backup sticks with them at every game.

A goalie's stick is slightly different. The bottom half is wider and ends in a paddle-like blade to give the goalie an even wider surface area, which they use to stop the puck from going into the goal.

Personalized for Players

Professional players typically have contracts with the companies that make hockey sticks and purchase those that have been made especially for them. Sticks are designated as either right-handed or left-handed, depending on whether a player shoots with their right or left hand; the blade curves accordingly in the same direction. For instance, if a player is a right-handed shooter, they will place their right hand one-third of the way down the shaft and hold the end of the stick with their left hand when making a shot.

Another factor that affects a player's selection is the amount of flexibility they want in the stick. For the most part, defensemen use a slightly stiffer stick; with less bend, they are better able to stick check their opponents and steal the puck. Forwards will typically use a more flexible shaft, which allows for quick and accurate wrist shots, as well as passing. In deciding on a stick's flexibility, a player also takes into account their size and weight. Stronger and heavier players generally prefer stiffer sticks that do not bend as much.

The top part of the stick is commonly wrapped with cloth tape that helps with the grip. The tape has adhesive on both sides; this makes it easier for the player to keep their grip on the stick. The blade is also wrapped with cloth tape. This is done to improve the handling of the puck as well as to prevent water damage to the blade if it is made of wood. The tape provides a rough surface, which is less slippery than a smooth one; this helps to create a straighter shot with less slipping off the center or toe of the blade. Additionally, the tape cushions the blade so that when a puck is passed, it does not bounce off.

Most professional hockey players work with designers to create a personalized hockey stick.

Changes to Blades

Until the middle of the 20th century, all hockey stick blades were straight. In the 1950s, Andy Bathgate of the New York Rangers created a curve in the blade and found he could make his slap shots more effective. In the 1960s, players Stan Mikita and Bobby Hull of the Chicago Blackhawks experimented with a broken blade and found it to be quite effective at hitting the puck. It was Mikita and Hull who popularized the curve of the blade even though others have claimed they experimented with it earlier. Alain Haché, author of *The Physics of Hockey*, explained,

> *The truth is, the curve is mostly about puck control, not puck speed. A curved blade makes the following three actions easier to achieve:*
>
> 1. ***Consistency**: the curve effectively forms a pocket at the bottom of which the puck will tend to go ...*
> 2. ***Control:** it's easier to scoop the puck and take it quickly around an opponent with a curved blade ...*
> 3. ***Puck spin:** it can hardly be seen by eye, but a curve permits more puck spin.*[1]

The curve of a hockey stick refers to the amount the blade curves from toe to heel (front to back). One of the most common curves is the toe curve, which is concentrated in the front end of the stick blade; this curve enables a player to handle the puck better and leads to more accurate wrist shots. A heel curve is more effective in slap shots.

Another differentiation is whether the stick blade is open or closed. An open blade means the face of the blade is turned up more sharply, while the closed blade is opposite. The more open a blade is, the easier it is to lift the puck, while a closed blade protects the puck.

1. Quoted in Jeremy Rupke, "Complete Guide to the Hockey Stick Curve," HowToHockey.com, August 18, 2010. howtohockey.com/hockey-stick-curve-guide/.

The Fastest Shot

Better sticks and blades have made shooting the puck easier and more efficient. One of the most effective of all hockey shots is the slap shot; it is momentum, motion, and speed that make this shot difficult to stop. Pucks, hit by such a shot, can travel at speeds up to 100 miles (161 km) per hour. This is one of the fastest shots in sports, although tennis balls and golf balls exceed the speed of a hockey puck. This shot is also one of the most exciting shots in the game of hockey.

Before All-Star games, players often participate in various competitions. These include speed skating, shooting the puck, and various maneuvering skills. Russian player Denis Kulyash set a new skills competition record for the fastest slap shot at the 2011 Kontinental Hockey League's All-Star game when his shot was clocked at 110.3 miles (177.5 km) per hour. Previously, Zdeno Chára of the Boston Bruins had the honor of taking the fastest slap shot with his 105.4-mile (169.7 km) per hour slap shot at the NHL's 2009 All-Star Game skills competition.

Most scientists believe that the slap shot is all about technique and energy transfer. This is what creates the power behind the shot. Journalist Kirsten Weir explained,

> *To prepare for the slap shot, a player twists at the waist as he swings the stick backward, then forward. That twisting action creates* angular momentum, *the momentum of a rotating object. The more momentum an object has, the harder it is to stop [and the faster it goes.] As the player strikes the puck, that angular momentum changes into* linear momentum, *driving the puck forward in a straight line.*[25]

During a slap shot, players hit the ice right before hitting the puck and then sweep the stick forward to make contact. When the stick first comes in contact with the ice, it bends because of its built-in

Japan's Sena Suzuki (#6) is shown here taking a slap shot during the Women's World Championship against Hungary on April 15, 2017, in Graz, Austria.

flexibility. This bow or bend in the stick creates more power because when the stick snaps back into position at puck contact, it releases energy into the puck, causing faster speeds.

To perform a slap shot, a player twists at the waist and shifts their weight from back to front; they also use a wrist snap. This snap creates spin off the stick, like a coiled spring that snaps. This wrist snap essentially produces a rotating action that keeps the puck stable and helps its accuracy.

In addition, the hockey stick absorbs less energy allowing more power to transfer to the puck. Weir explained, "Every time a player hits the puck, energy passes from the athlete to the stick to the puck."[26]

Less Powerful but Still Effective Shots

Other hockey shots are not quite as powerful as the slap shot. Another popular and effective shot is the wrist shot, made with a flick of the wrist. This shot is different than the slap shot in that it lacks the wind-up that is used in performing the slap shot; in addition, the puck is in contact with the stick blade for a slightly longer period of time. This gives the player more control over the direction of the puck.

Brenden Morrow, formerly a left wing player and captain of the Dallas Stars, said, "Probably the biggest advantage of a wrist shot is accuracy over power. If you want to get something done quick, you can just take a quick wrist shot that's very accurate."[27] Dr. Robert Gehrz of the University of Minnesota explained, "The wrist shot is the most accurate shot in hockey because the player can direct the puck exactly where he or she wants it to go. And this is done by a combination of carefully pointing the stick when you shoot in the right direction and putting the spin on the puck to keep it stable as it's flying."[28]

The one-timer is another shot that has the potential to be hit with a lot of power. This shot occurs when one player passes the puck to another and the second player makes a shot immediately. In this case, the second player winds up before the puck arrives and then quickly redirects the puck toward the net. Capable of nearly reaching the speed of a slap shot, the one-timer shot is difficult to stop because of the quickness with which it is hit. The rapid change in direction not only adds extra energy to the shot, but it is also often hard for the goalie to follow.

The Goaltender

The goaltender is responsible for stopping all shots before they enter the net. A goalie has a number of ways to stop the puck. The most common way is stopping it with the body, resulting in the puck bouncing off the goalie's padding and away from the net. They can also use the oversize catching glove to actually catch the puck or to reject the puck with the stick.

Science helps explain how goalies are able to stop so many shots from getting past them and into the goal.

All of these methods require speed and agility on the part of the goaltender. Reaction time and mental preparation are the key components for a successful goaltender. The Science of Hockey website states, "In a game where the puck travels at high speeds, the difference between a goal and a save can come down to milliseconds."[29]

Many players believe that the best goaltenders have natural ability and quickness. Many scientists agree, arguing that reaction time is a genetic trait. However, most goaltenders, with or without this genetic trait, can improve their ability to react quickly through practice.

In such a high-speed sport as hockey, a goalie's reflexes are also crucial in protecting the goal. If a puck is shot from the blue line, which is 64 feet (19.5 m) away from the goal, at 100 miles (161 km) per hour, the puck will reach the goaltender in less than 1 second. This does not allow the goalie much time to block the shot. Several factors can impact the goaltender's success and improve their reaction time. The first is just being in the right place at the right time. Sometimes, this is the result of luck, but typically, it is because the goaltender is paying attention to where the puck is at all times.

Pucks often travel faster than the naked eye can track. It is, therefore, amazing that most goaltenders are able to stop nearly 90 percent of the shots that are directed at the goal. Science writer Charles Q. Choi explained, "To do so, the best athletes rely on what researcher Joan Vickers at the University of Calgary dubbed 'the quiet eye,' the critical moment of focus prior to action."[30]

To observe this phenomenon, researchers inserted a camera in goaltenders' helmets and followed their eye movements during a game. According to Choi, the researchers discovered that "elite goalies focused directly on the puck nearly a full second before the shot was released nearly three-quarters of the time. They also concentrated on the ice in front of the stick when it came to a quarter of all shots. Their gaze was only on the body of the shooter two percent of the time."[31] This ability to see the puck before a shot is taken speeds up the reaction time and allows the goaltender to stop a speeding puck. Researchers also found that new or novice goaltenders allowed their eyes to wander over the ice; this lessened their chances of stopping the puck. Thus, experience and practice play a significant role in the ability of goaltenders to prevent scoring.

To be at their best, goaltenders also have to be well prepared mentally. During pregame warm-up drills, goalies practice taking shots from their teammates. Concentrating on preventing the pucks from reaching the goal helps the goalies sharpen their mental capacities. They also "stop" imaginary shots by crouching down in front of the net and moving from side to side. This further sharpens their mental processes.

Another factor that can help goalies be more effective is the concept of being "in the zone." Ottawa Senators goalie Craig Anderson explained, "You take the mind out of it, just read and react … You just want to take ice, and make sure I didn't give him an easy shot. By taking ice, you force him to maybe do something he didn't want to do. If you start thinking about shoulda, coulda, woulda, or maybe he might do this, you usually second guess yourself."[32]

University of Connecticut (UConn) Women's Ice Hockey team goaltender Annie Belanger (#41) is shown here keeping Boston University players away from the net. A goalie's ability to follow the puck at all times is essential in preventing a goal.

Chapter 4

Avoiding Injuries

According to a 2016 IIHF survey, over 1.7 million people around the world play on registered ice hockey teams, and that number does not include children or adults who play informally. Due to the fast nature of the sport, almost every one of these players will probably sustain at least one injury during their time playing hockey. Also because of the nature of the sport, many of these injuries cannot be avoided entirely.

The Sports Injury Clinic, a website that provides information on a wide variety of sports injuries and treatment, states, "Ice hockey is a dangerous sport due to the high speeds, slippery surface, sharp blades and a solid puck traveling at up to 100 miles per hour."[33] The Centers for Disease Control and Prevention (CDC) states that hockey players are more at risk for concussions than participants in any other sport.

What can be done to reduce the number of these serious injuries? According to experts, "Wearing properly fitted safety equipment and gear can reduce the severity and incidence of the most common hockey injuries. The well-dressed hockey player wears head-to-toe protection including certified safety equipment and well-fitting gear."[34]

Additionally, experts suggest that to minimize injury risk,

> *A helmet should fit snugly and have an adjustable chin strap [to] keep the helmet from moving forward, backward or side to side. Always wear a face shield or mask with your helmet … Mouth guards help reduce the risk of injury to the face, jaw, mouth and teeth … The most effective mouth guards fit well and are comfortable,*

but they also stay in place, are durable, easy to clean and don't restrict speaking and breathing.[35]

Protective Gear

Since there is a high risk of injury, all hockey players wear layers of protective gear. Shoulder pads, chest protectors, leg and shin guards, helmets, and gloves all help protect from possible injury. Of all the players on the ice, the goaltender is probably the most at risk due to their responsibility for stopping the puck. In the early days of hockey, goalies wore no protective equipment. This left them vulnerable to concussions, facial cuts, nasal fractures, and other injuries.

In the last several decades, however, innovations and changes in goalie equipment have made the goalie's job a bit easier. Designed to protect the goalie from the speed and dangers of the puck, the goalie's equipment is different than the rest of the players on the ice. Most goalie equipment weighs around 50 pounds (23 kg), as compared to the 20 pounds (9 kg) worn by other players.

A goaltender's pads, for instance, are much thicker than those worn by their teammates, because the goalie faces the majority of shots. In addition, the goalie wears large pads on their legs on top of their hockey uniform that reach nearly to the groin. Oversize gloves protect the hands catching and blocking the puck. Goalies also have large helmets with face masks.

All players, regardless of age, wear protective gear including helmets and shin guards. They also wear chest protectors under their shirts.

According to hockey historian Douglas Hunter, "no [other] role in team sport has such violence associated with it. Injury, now much less a part of goaltending with advances in equipment, is an essential part of its lore … The goaltender alone dresses for the worst. He is sheathed in more paraphernalia [protective gear] than a medieval knight, deliberately placing himself in the path of a chunk of vulcanized rubber hurtling at more than 100 miles per hour."[36]

Goalies also wear skates with hard plastic shells, a heavy chest protector, and heavy elbow and shoulder pads. This padding is made out of synthetic materials, which provide more strength and less absorbency than the old leather padding worn by hockey players of the past.

PLAYER *and* GOALIE *gear*

From Plastic Shells to the Birdcage: Evolution of the Goalie's Mask

Until 1959, goaltenders did not wear masks. A facial injury to goaltender Jacques Plante compelled him to try a simple plastic shell to protect his face. Plastic masks soon led to the invention of a simple fiberglass one. Years would pass, however, before goalie masks became standard equipment.

One of the reasons for the slow acceptance of masks was the difficulty with which they were made. Hunter explained, "Having a custom-fitted mask made meant subjecting yourself to the creation of a head mold. This entailed tugging a woman's stocking over your head, then being smeared with vaseline and coated with plaster—and breathing through a straw so you didn't suffocate."[1] When made, the fiberglass masks were white in color and rather plain in appearance. Goalies began painting their personal masks with different colors and symbols.

A serious eye injury to former Buffalo Sabres goalie Gerry Desjardins, who was wearing a fiberglass mask in 1977, helped start the movement toward a new and safer kind of mask. The birdcage mask, which is worn by goalies today, was developed in the 1970s. With a helmet made of fiberglass or Kevlar (the same material used in bulletproof vests) and layers of internal padding, at least 0.63-inch (1.6 cm) thick, covering the head, the mask part is similar to that worn by a baseball catcher. These masks and helmets offer solid protection from fast-flying pucks. Each top goalie in the NHL has one or more personalized masks. NHL goalie Marc-Andre Fleury said, "You always try to find something to represent the city and yourself, to look good from far away and close up."[2]

NHL goalies typically wear personalized and creative birdcage facemasks.

1. Douglas Hunter, *A Breed Apart: An Illustrated History of Goaltending*. Chicago: Benchmark, 1995, p. 127.
2. Quoted in Jason Mackey, "Mask Painting Allows Hockey Goalies Freedom of Expression," Pittsburgh Post-Gazette, October 16, 2016. www.post-gazette.com/sports/penguins/2016/10/16/Mask-painting-allows-hockey-goalies-freedom-of-expression/stories/201610160082.

Some of the padding is made with a product called Dri-FIT, which is made by Nike. According to Nike, "Nike Dri-FIT is a high-performance, microfiber, polyester fabric that moves sweat away from the body and to the fabric surface, where it evaporates. As a result, Dri-FIT keeps athletes dry and comfortable. Dri-FIT technology is used in a variety of Nike products, including shirts, socks, pants, shorts … and more."[37] Dri-FIT and other similar products make use of water-repelling microfibers that are made of polyester and nylon. The fibers are so small that moisture has a difficult time getting through them.

Power Play

David Gunnarsson is one of the most popular goalie mask painters—more than half of the NHL's goalies use him. His work includes the New York Rangers logo and Statue of Liberty on Henrik Lundqvist's New York Rangers mask, Batman on Frederik Anderson's Toronto Maple Leafs mask, and the chewing ice monster on Jason Kasdorf's Buffalo Sabres mask.

A Crucial Invention

Perhaps no innovation in ice hockey has been as important as the goalie mask. Gary Abraham said, "Goalies are more susceptible to injuries around the neck from pucks, skates, and sticks."[38] However, it took many years before players even considered wearing a protective mask and helmet.

In the early days of hockey, the goaltender was at high risk for injuries simply because of the lack of body and head protection. Fast-flying pucks that were not caught could easily cause facial lacerations, bruises, and other injuries. These injuries could also occur to other parts of the body as well. Collisions with other players who slid into the net could produce broken bones, while the skates of an out-of-control player could easily cause severe cuts. Goalies also had more concussions because of falls or shots to the head. With as many as 40 shots heading toward a goal during a game, goalie injuries were almost inevitable.

Clint Benedict, a Montreal Maroons goaltender, had his nose and cheekbone injured in 1930. After that, he tried wearing a leather mask he made that covered his whole face except his eyes. However, he found it hard to see through it and around it, and he eventually stopped wearing it. No other kind of helmet or mask was used for almost 30 years. As a hockey coach, Benedict later discovered a young goalie in Winnipeg named Roy Mosgrove who was using a wire-cage protector similar to what catchers wear in baseball. Hunter wrote, "It would take decades for the players … to see the wisdom of Roy Mosgrove, and to incorporate the wire cage into mask design."[39]

Jacques Plante of the Montreal Canadiens finally modernized the goalie mask as a result of an injury he sustained. On November 1, 1959, Plante suffered a cut to his nose and cheek while blocking a shot from Andy Bathgate of the New York Rangers. Blood streamed down his face as he returned to the bench. Plante told his coach that he would no longer be playing goalie unless he could wear some kind of mask and protection. The coach allowed Plante to wear a thin, skin-colored fiberglass shell to protect his face.

When asked about his mask, Plante said, "When I first put on the mask, the boys all told me I would scare the women. They wouldn't come to see the games anymore. I'll tell you something, if I went on the way I was going, pretty soon my face would look worse than the mask."[40]

Goalie Jacques Plante wore a mask during games to protect his face from injuries.

Lacerations, Sprains, and Other Injuries

Despite the advances in hockey equipment, injuries still occur with alarming frequency. Many hockey players suffer from various cuts, or lacerations, to their body from a puck, hockey stick, or skate. Sports medicine physicians estimate that almost half of all hockey injuries are lacerations.

Most of these injuries are treated by the team trainer and stitched in the dressing room during the game. Deeper cuts may require further treatment and more stitches. The late Terry Sawchuk, who played for several NHL teams over 16 years, needed more than 400 stitches total during his career.

Another common ice hockey injury is a sprained or strained muscle. A sprain is an injury to a ligament—the tissue that holds bones together at the joints—whereas a strain is an injury to a muscle or tendon. Tendons connect muscle to bone; a tear in the tendon or muscle can be painful.

Injuries can happen due to a fall, a blow, or even a simple misstep. This can

The Injured List

Hockey injuries are quite common, but just how common? During the 2016–2017 season, many players were on the NHL's injured list. Several notable players suffered serious injuries that took them out for many games. These injuries ranged from concussions to lower-body injuries to broken hands and more. Most injuries were minor, and the players were expected to return to action in a matter of days. Several of the injuries, however, were more severe.

The Buffalo Sabres were especially hit hard with injuries to key players Ryan O'Reilly, Tyler Ennis, Evander Kane, and Jack Eichel. Before the season opener, Eichel suffered a high ankle sprain and did not return to the ice until the end of November.

The Tampa Bay Lightning also suffered a significant loss with Steven Stamkos's torn lateral meniscus in his right knee in November. Stamkos, center and captain of the Tampa Bay Lightning, was out the rest of the season.

On November 18, 2016, Brad Richardson of the Arizona Coyotes was carried off the ice on a stretcher due to a fractured tibia and fibula, and he was sidelined for the remainder of the season.

Players unable to play due to injury can have a serious negative effect on a professional hockey team. This can severely impact a team's performance and the chance of winning and making the playoffs.

result in a sprain, during which the ligaments that hold the bones together are torn. Numerous small blood vessels are also damaged which allows blood to get into the surrounding tissue, causing the area to swell. All strains and sprains are caused by excessive use or tension on a particular body part or a blow that increases this tension.

Treatment of a sprain or strain is compression of the area with a bandage and the application of ice. Both limit the amount of swelling. The bandage also limits movement, allowing the torn muscle to repair itself.

Contusions, or bruises, are nearly everyday occurrences in ice hockey. A contusion is a discoloration of the skin caused by bleeding into the muscle or skin and follows a fall, hard hit, or other injury. It is treated with ice, compression, elevation, and rest.

Ice is applied every few hours for no more than 20 minutes at a time; ice causes the blood vessels to contract, which slows down any bleeding into the tissue. It lessens swelling and inflammation by reducing the amount of fluid released from injured tissue that occurs automatically in response to an injury. The injured body part is also elevated to decrease swelling, as gravity will drain accumulated fluid away from the injury.

Lower back injuries are also part of hockey. Most involve some damage to the discs that lie between each vertebra. Discs rupture and can become compressed due to the bent-over position that hockey players skate and play in, along with their frequent collisions with other players and the boards.

The loss of teeth used to be more common in ice hockey than it is today. Players now wear mouth guards that protect them from having teeth knocked out. Still, it is not unusual to see players with one or more teeth missing.

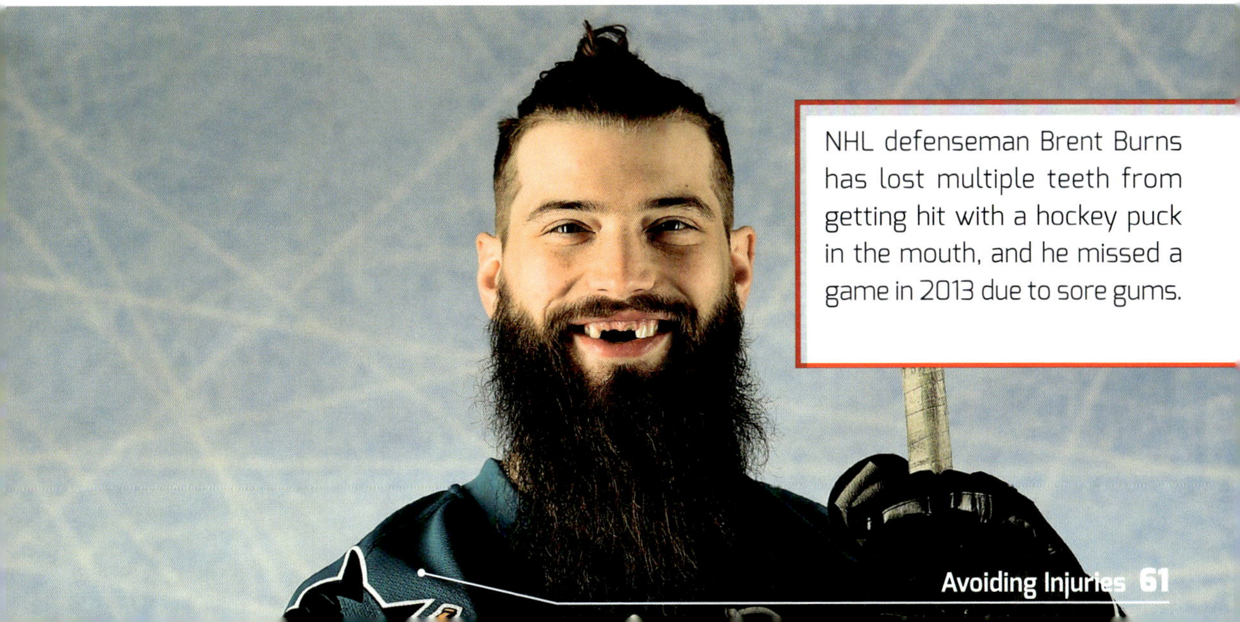

NHL defenseman Brent Burns has lost multiple teeth from getting hit with a hockey puck in the mouth, and he missed a game in 2013 due to sore gums.

Facial cuts and fractures are also part of hockey. These have decreased somewhat in recent years due to more players wearing visors to protect part of their face. Visors are available; however, many players refuse to wear them because they say that the visors impair their vision.

Damaged Knees

Knee injuries occur frequently in ice hockey and are more serious than simple lacerations and strains. Richard Mangi, Peter Jokl, and O. William Dayton, authors of the book *Sports Fitness and Training*, explained, "Hockey is a rough game. The swift cuts and turns, the flying bodies, and sudden trips are unhealthy for … knees."[41]

The knee, which acts like a hinge, is designed to be flexible and provide stability for walking. The knee is where the major bones of the leg meet; the femur from above, and the tibia and fibula from below. The bones' meeting place is protected by another bone called the patella, or kneecap.

To provide further support, thick ligaments hold the bones together. The two collateral and two cruciate ligaments add stability, with the collateral ligaments providing sideways stability. In addition, the knee is also filled with shock-absorbing cartilage, lubricating membranes, and sacs called bursas whose purpose is to reduce friction and cushion the area between bones and tendons. Any of these knee components can be injured, especially when the leg or knee is hit hard.

The most common knee injury occurs when one of the major ligaments is sprained or torn. The most often damaged ligament is the medial collateral ligament (MCL). A blow to the outside of the knee can sprain this ligament, especially when the foot is planted on the ice when the hit occurs. The blow causes the knee to move unnaturally and places strain on the ligament, often resulting in a tear. The treatment of choice for this injury is rest, compression, and ice.

Power Play

Bill Masterton is the only player in the NHL to die from an injury sustained during a game; he died from a massive brain hemorrhage after falling backward onto the ice on January 13, 1968.

A more serious injury is a tear in the anterior cruciate ligament (ACL). This kind of injury occurs when the hit is more severe or if the hockey player's knee rotates too much. If this ligament is torn, the player will often hear a loud pop followed by severe pain and an inability to stand or place weight on the leg. The loud pop is caused by the actual tearing of the ligament. When it tears, the action is similar to the snap of a taut rubber band and produces a loud pop.

A torn ACL can be a career-ending injury, typically requiring surgery to repair the torn ligament. The ACL is

ANATOMY *of the* KNEE JOINT

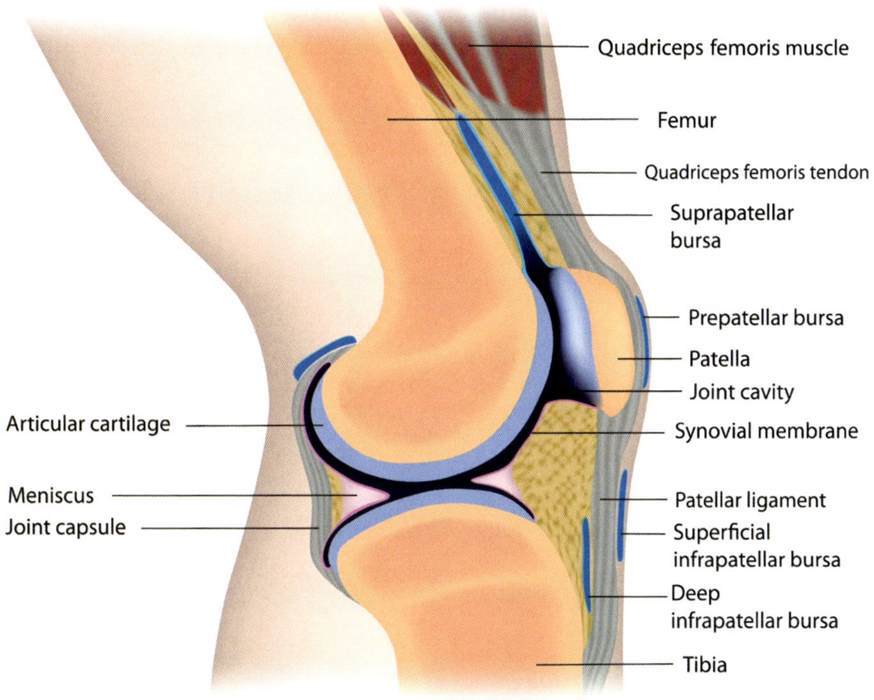

The knee acts like a hinge and consists of multiple muscles, tendons, and ligaments, which are shown here.

the main stabilizer of the knee and is crucial to proper knee and leg function. An injury to this important ligament is often accompanied by injury to other ligaments and muscles in the knee, thus making recovery and repair of the injury much more difficult. Surgery is followed by five to six months of rehabilitation to strengthen the knee. In February 2017, St. Louis Blues forward Robby Fabbri suffered an ACL tear and missed the rest of the season.

Head Injuries

While the use of helmets has decreased the incidence of concussions, this potentially severe injury to the brain is not uncommon in ice hockey. Helmets do not prevent the kinds of whiplash injuries that can shake the brain back and forth within the skull, causing a concussion.

According to Allan M. Levy and Mark L. Fuerst, authors of *Sports Injury Handbook*, "a concussion is any loss of consciousness, even for a moment, or disorientation after a blow to the head."[42] Mangi, Jokl, and Dayton explained,

> *A concussion literally means violent shaking of the brain. A blow to the head causes rapid acceleration and deceleration of the brain as it smacks against the skull on the side opposite to the blow. The brain and meninges [the lining of the brain] are injured, with bleeding into the brain and death of individual brain cells. There is a temporary disruption of the brain's normal functions, a scrambling of circuits, and a transient impairment of mental function.*[43]

Most concussions occur because of collisions, either with another player or the boards. For example, Zdeno Chára of the Boston Bruins checked Montreal Canadiens' Max Pacioretty, causing him to collide with a glass partition in a game on March 8, 2011. It resulted in a concussion and broken vertebrae that kept him out of the rest of that season.

Physicians generally grade concussions on a scale of 1 to 3, with 3 being the most serious. A player may be unconscious for several minutes from a grade 3 concussion. Individuals with a grade 3 concussion generally suffer severe confusion and dizziness, and the rate of recovery is slow. If a player is knocked out, they are kept immobile and a neck brace is placed on them to prevent the possibility of neck injury. "Any player who loses consciousness," Mangi, Jokl, and Dayton wrote, "should be sent to the hospital for evaluation."[44]

Occasionally a hard blow to the head can also fracture the bones of the skull. These fractures, which are typically depressed, causing the bones to press into the brain, can put pressure on the brain or tear blood vessels. This is a serious injury, which can lead to a comatose state or even death. As a result, any blow to the head is treated as potentially life threatening.

A player who suffers a grade 1 or 2 concussion may be stunned for a few seconds and have trouble remembering where they are or what they are doing. In this level of head injury, there is typically no loss of consciousness. Players may have brief confusion, some temporary memory loss, and mild dizziness. Recovery from this type of concussion is generally fairly quick.

No concussion, however, should be treated lightly. Abraham explained,

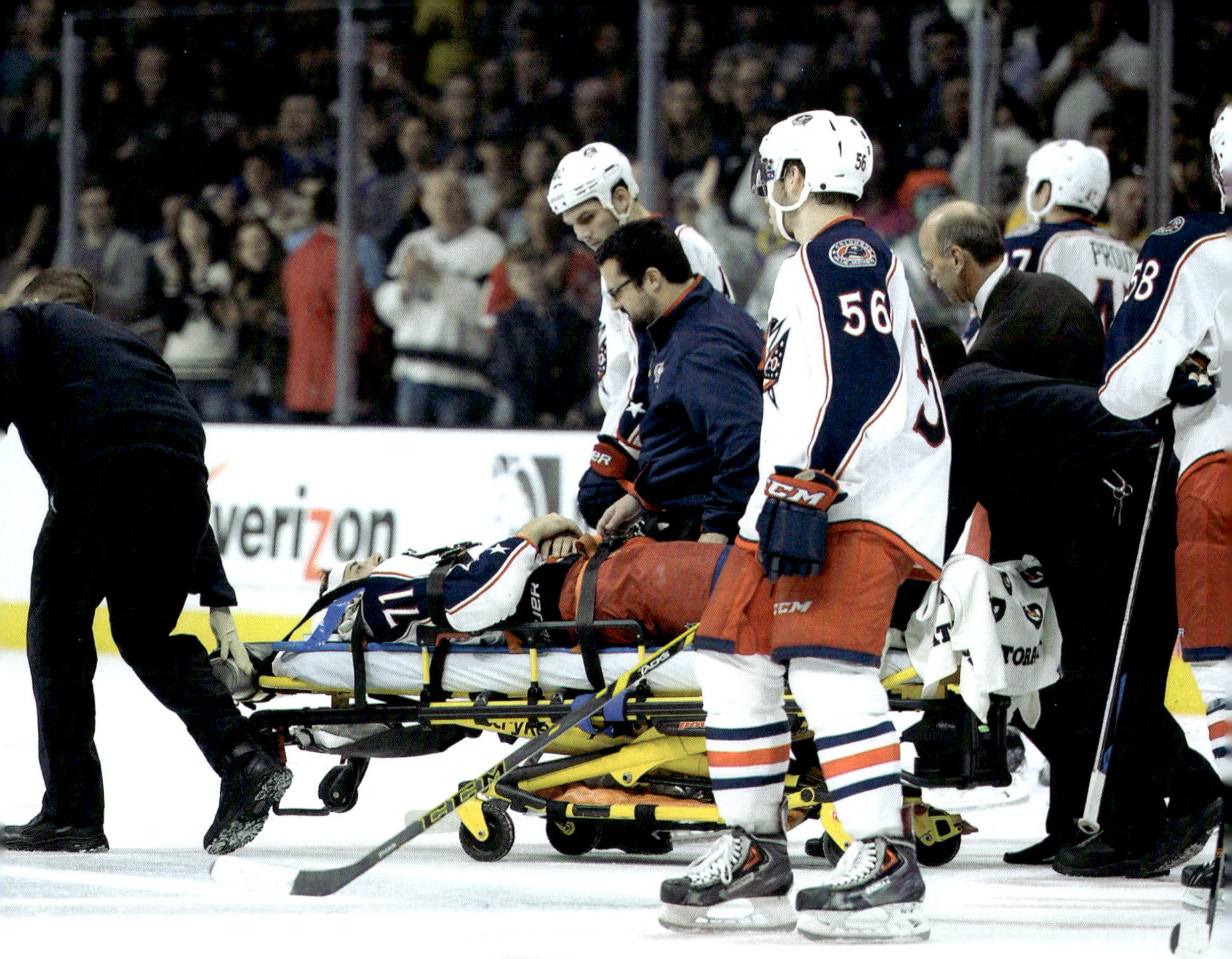

Injuries can sometimes require that the player be hospitalized.

"Any concussion is cause for concern. Even the ringing sensation after a collision or blow to the head—what used to be called 'having your bell rung'—should be taken seriously."[45] A ringing sensation, called tinnitus, following a head injury often indicates the possibility of internal injury to the brain.

The treatment for a concussion is rest to give the brain time to heal. Players are evaluated by a neurologist, a doctor who specializes in the nervous system, and tested extensively for severity of injury. These tests may include a computed (or computerized) tomography (CT) scan of the brain or a magnetic resonance imaging (MRI) scan to determine the extent of any brain injury. Both tests utilize X-rays to visualize brain or other tissue. A CT scan provides a three-dimensional image of the brain. As the patient lies in the scanner, the X-ray machine moves across the patient, taking a slice-by-slice picture of the brain. An MRI utilizes similar technology but provides a greater contrast between the different tissues in body parts, thus creating a better and more detailed picture of the problem.

In the first few hours after a concussion, doctors watch injured players carefully for any signs of severe headache, nausea, vomiting, and further loss of consciousness. All of these symptoms can be signs of internal bleeding.

Players in the NHL are not allowed to play again until all of their symptoms are gone. Sometimes this takes a few days, and sometimes it takes a few months. Some players suffer from post-concussion syndrome and experience headaches, fatigue, dizziness, and impaired concentration or memory. Players must pass an extensive neurological exam before returning to the ice. This exam includes checks on a player's reflexes, muscle strength, balance, and the pressure in the back of the eyes.

Life-Threatening Injuries

Most injuries in ice hockey are not immediately life threatening. Occasionally, however, catastrophic injuries do occur. Richard Zednik, a former player for the Florida Panthers hockey team, was playing the Buffalo Sabres in Buffalo,

Craig Cunningham

Sometimes players have injuries or other medical emergencies that occur at the arena, or even on the ice, but not during a game. This situation happened to Tucson Roadrunners center Craig Cunningham on November 19, 2016. Cunningham was on the ice before the game started when he had a seizure and fell. Medical personnel cut his jersey and performed emergency CPR while he was still on the ice. Cunningham was taken out on a stretcher and then transferred from a local hospital to a medical center that was better able to assist him. Later reports confirmed that he suffered a heart attack at just 26 years old. One of the doctors stated that his heart was not beating without assistance for several days after the heart attack.

About a month later, Cunningham put out a statement of thanks from his hospital bed. "I wouldn't be here today without these doctors, our trainers, and the firefighters who were at the arena that night."[1]

Cunningham said that while he probably will not play professional hockey anymore, he does want to stay involved with the sport at some level.

1. Quoted in Liam McGuire, "Craig Cunningham Speaks out on Near-Death Incident, Says He's Likely Done with Hockey," Puck Drunk Love, December 21, 2016. thecomeback.com/puckdrunklove/nhl/craig-cunningham-speaks-out-on-near-death-incident-says-hes-likely-done-with-hockey.html.

New York, on February 10, 2008. One of his teammates tripped over the leg of an opposing player and slid into Zednik, cutting his neck with his skate blade. Zednik, despite the severe injury, had the instinct to grab his neck and immediately skate to his bench, leaving a trail of blood behind on the ice. Journalist Steve Milton wrote,

> *With nine minutes and 56 seconds left in an intensely played game bearing serious playoff implications, Zednik drifted behind the Buffalo net and into a small scrum of players in the corner. Florida captain Olli Jokinen was upended and, as he fell, the razor sharp edge of his skate blade ran across the right side of Zednik's throat, slicing into the common carotid artery, the oxygen highway to the brain.*[46]

An injury to the common carotid artery is a catastrophic injury because this particular artery is a large vessel that carries blood and oxygen to the brain. Fortunately, Zednik received immediate medical attention from Florida trainer Dave Zenobi and other medical personnel in the arena.

One of the medical professionals who responded was Les Bisson, a team doctor for the Buffalo Sabres and an expert in catastrophic injuries. Using a rolled up towel to apply pressure to the injury, Bisson was able to control much of the bleeding until Zednik reached a hospital. From the time of the injury to Zednik's arrival at the hospital, only 10 minutes passed. Bisson later stated, "This is one you hope would never happen. In a significant vascular injury scenario, the goal is to control it with pressure and get to an ambulance as quickly as humanly possible."[47]

Doctors reported that Zednik lost 5 pints (2,366 ml) of blood. (The average human blood supply is 1.2 to 1.5 gallons, or 4.7 to 5.5 liters.) Doctors also noted that if the artery had been completely severed, rather than just cut, Zednik could have died. Physicians later credited Zednik's quick thinking and his determination to get to the bench as factors that helped save his life. In addition, medical personnel at the arena were praised for their quick and proper attention and treatment.

After a brief hospitalization, Zednik was released and placed on the team's injury list. Zednik retired in 2009, shortly after coming back to the game. Efforts to require hockey players to wear neck guards that help prevent injuries such as this in the NHL have failed. Reporter Sarah Larimer explained, "The NHL always has had a macho culture. Goalies didn't regularly wear facemasks until the 1960s and helmets weren't mandated for incoming players until 11 years after Minnesota North Star Bill Masterton died from striking his head on the ice in 1968."[48]

Holt Bennington is another hockey player who suffered a catastrophic injury. Bennington, a high school sophomore defenseman, was playing in a junior-varsity game in January 1998 when he

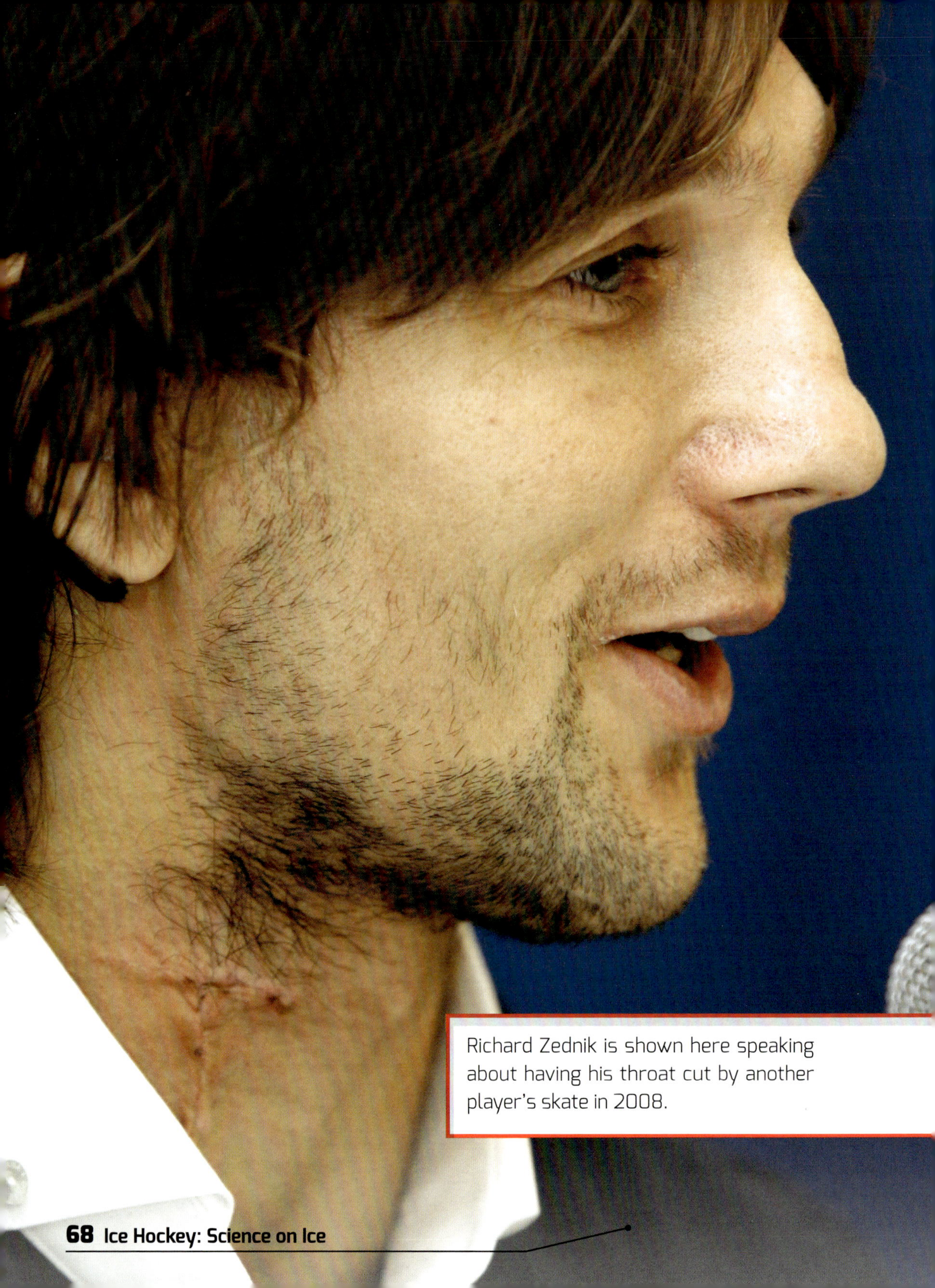

Richard Zednik is shown here speaking about having his throat cut by another player's skate in 2008.

suffered a severe injury to his cervical spine that caused a fracture between the fifth and sixth vertebrae in his neck. The injury occurred when he slammed headfirst into the boards.

Even though he was conscious and alert, Bennington could not move his arms or legs and was carried off the ice on a stretcher, fully immobilized. His coach, Ed Loiselle, called it a freak accident. Abraham explained, "Classically, a neck injury occurs when a player is hit from behind, flies into the boards and hits the top of the helmet against the boards with the neck bent forward."[49]

Following surgery to stabilize the fracture, Bennington was transferred to a long-term rehabilitation hospital. Initially, doctors were hopeful that the young man would regain some use of his arms and legs, but his rehabilitation was unsuccessful, and he is a quadriplegic.

Players Getting Even

Many catastrophic injuries are caused by fighting between players. When a player is injured by an opposing player during the game, his teammates often feel the need to retaliate, or "get even." Often, there is retribution during the same game or in the next game played against the team and player who caused the injury. While coaches and players generally deny any allegations of retaliation on the ice, according to the Sports Ethicist, "Fighting is [seen as] necessary in the NHL because it allows the players to police the sport through retaliation for egregious play by opponents."[50]

Such an incident occurred between the Boston Bruins and the Pittsburgh Penguins on December 7, 2013. Shawn Thornton, a player for the Bruins, knocked Penguins player Brooks Orpik to the ground and punched him repeatedly. Orpik had to be removed via stretcher, while Thornton received a 15-game suspension. Thornton said it was in retaliation for earlier in the game, when James Neal of the Penguins had given Bruins player Brad Marchand a knee to the head while Marchand was already down on the ice, and Orpik had earlier given a concussion to Bruins player Loui Eriksson.

Another incident occurred on March 8, 2016. Darnell Nurse of the Edmonton Oilers repeatedly punched Roman Polak of the San Jose Sharks. The punches were in apparent retaliation for an accidental crash between Polak and Oilers' forward Matt Hendricks. According to the NHL's Department of Player Safety, the collision was accidental, and Polak did not attempt to hit back when Nurse attacked him. Nurse was suspended for three games and had to give $13,924.74 of his salary to the Players' Emergency Assistance Fund.

Unfortunately, these are not isolated incidents. Retaliation is a problem that the NHL has been unable to completely stop. Stiff penalties and suspensions are handed out, but in the heat and intensity of a game, such hits occur.

The Stress of the Game

Injuries, severe or otherwise, add up. Hockey is a rough game, and the body of a hockey player takes the brunt of the roughness. Howard Green, a professor at the University of Waterloo in Ontario, Canada, said, "Hockey is uniquely stressful … the heat and humidity of the protective gear, the high level of coordination required, the repeated demands made on the muscles with little rest and the astounding requirement that it's played while balancing on skate blades are all factors [in fatigue]."[51]

Trainer Rick Burrill said, "Hitting the boards sounds good in the stands. The fans love it and they rationalize it by saying it isn't as bad as it looks. They're right. It's not as bad as it looks each time. But they all add up. After a while, you end up with some kind of degenerative, arthritic condition that keeps you from playing competitive hockey."[52]

In a 2013 study titled "I Went to a Fight the Other Night and a Hockey Game Broke Out," researchers Nadav Goldschmied and Samantha Espindola looked at the reasons why hockey players fight. They observed the games of the 2010–2011 season and found that players fought more at the beginning of a game than at the end. They also analyzed data from 2000–2011 and found that the least amount of violence took place during the postseason. They concluded that "players take into account the penalties associated with fighting and are less likely to engage in violence when the stakes are high, such as at the end of a game or season … The findings suggest that a more punitive system should diminish fighting behavior markedly."[53]

Injuries are a frightening part of hockey, which is why wearing the right safety gear and training properly is so important.

Proper Conditioning

In the early days of professional hockey, players spent a few weeks before the season warming up by playing practice games. Not much time or thought was given to year-round conditioning. The 1960s ushered in a general "Fitness Fever," with many men and women beginning exercise programs, flocking to new health clubs, and joining amateur sports teams. To serve the needs of these exercise buffs, the field of sports medicine began.

Professional athletes also began questioning how they could minimize or prevent certain injuries, as well as how they could increase their stamina. Team trainers and coaches went searching for answers to help their players.

Peter Twist, former strength and conditioning coach for the Vancouver Canucks, now owns and operates an athletic conditioning company. He advocates combining hockey techniques with fitness exercises. As a result, "hockey players are able to build lean muscle mass, size, and strength in a functional, whole-body manner that improves transfer to on-ice performance and better expresses the strength gained in the weight room in game action."[54]

Taking a Toll

Ice hockey is one of the most demanding sports in terms of the toll it takes on a player's body. Exhaustion is always a problem due to the fast-paced nature of the sport. Alain Haché, author of *The Physics of Hockey*, explained,

> *Hockey players move faster on their feet than athletes of any other team sport; some NHL players skate at speeds in excess of 25 mph (40 km/h or 11 m/s) . . . The legendary Bobby Hull, the*

fastest skater of his time, was once clocked at 29.2 mph, or 47 km/h. After Hull had spent 29 minutes on the ice during one game, sports scientists figured out that he had skated over 13 km … It is not surprising that during 60 minutes of regulation time a player will burn as many as 6,000 calories and lose up to 15 pounds.[55]

Because of these high demands, most hockey players stay on the ice for periods of only 30 to 80 seconds. Former defenseman Doug Bodger explained why the short periods are necessary: "I don't think you're breathing half the time. You're mostly exhaling … pushing and shoving … and concentrating so much you don't think about breathing at all. That's why we can only stay out there for a minute at a time. It's like holding your breath."[56]

On average, hockey players are on the ice between 15 and 20 minutes in an average 60-minute game. During that time, they are skating at peak speeds and making aggressive body contact with other players. This kind of

From the early days of the sport, hockey has been physically punishing for those who play it.

performance requires players to be in top physical shape. Endurance is an important factor. The goal is for a player to be able to perform at the same high level at the end of the game as at the beginning. To do this, a player must be in peak physical condition.

Much of this conditioning takes place in the off-season as players prepare to face a long and exhausting season. Eighty-two games are held in the regular season, and there are additional games for the teams that make it to the Stanley Cup playoffs. The season begins in October and can last until June.

To make it through long games and a long season, hockey players must stay in peak physical condition. Wayne Gretzky explained, "For a better conditioned athlete there is less chance of injury, and conditioning promotes career longevity. The player also becomes mentally stronger, after enduring the intense efforts required for conditioning."[57]

Power Play

As of 2017, 4 goalies have celebrated more than 300 regular season victories with the only team they have ever played on: Henrik Lundqvist of the New York Rangers; Mike Richter, who retired with the New York Rangers; Turk Broda, who retired with the Toronto Maple Leafs; and Marc-Andre Fleury of the Pittsburgh Penguins.

Muscle Function

A hockey player's strength, skill, and endurance depend on well-developed and healthy muscles. The human body has more than 600 different muscles, each of which is responsible for a specific task. Some muscles work alone, but the majority work together in groups. The primary function of muscles is to provide motion, but muscles also protect vital organs from injury. Muscles are also responsible for certain metabolic actions that occur each day, such as the beating of the heart, breathing, and the digestion of food.

There are three different kinds of muscles in every human body: smooth, cardiac, and skeletal. Smooth muscle can be found in the stomach and intestines, while cardiac muscle is heart muscle. Skeletal muscle is by far the most common. Skeletal muscles are attached to the bones and provide motion. They are called voluntary muscles, because they are controlled by the brain in a conscious process.

Muscles provide movement by contracting and then relaxing. Myosin and actin, two bands of protein, play major roles in the contraction of skeletal muscle. The brain, spinal cord, and nerves also help the muscles work. The nerves connect the brain and spinal cord to the various muscles with nerve fibers called neurons. These neurons form a network through which nerve impulses travel from one synapse or contact point to another by way of the release of various chemicals. To bend the knee, for example, the brain sends a chemical message down the spinal cord and then through the nerve transmission lines into the muscles surrounding the knee. As a result of these transmissions, the knee then bends. In fact, a message along one nerve can affect as many as 100 small muscles. The body's muscles act like a machine by using energy efficiently and producing muscle activity.

Muscles can perform a variety of tasks. There are straightening muscles, such as the biceps in the arm, that help the arm straighten after bending; to bend the arm, the other large muscle, the triceps, is used. The triceps is a bending muscle. Other muscles are classified as flexors; these bring adjacent body parts together. Extensors then move them apart. Abductor muscles move the arm away from the body, while adductors move it back. Pronator muscles help turn a body part, such as turning the hand face up, while supinator muscles turn body parts down. Finally rotator muscles, such as those in the hip and shoulder, help a body part rotate. Most muscles are arranged in pairs, with one doing the contracting and the other doing the relaxing.

Connective Tissue

Each muscle is surrounded by a sheath of connective tissue that encloses it, supports it, and connects it to other body parts. One example of connective tissue is the tendon, a strong band of tissue that connects muscle to bone. Tendons are tough but also elastic and can be strengthened by exercise. They are also one of the body parts most subject to stress and inflammation, especially in a high-energy sport such as ice hockey.

Ligaments are thinner bands of fibrous tissue; these connect bones to joints. Ligaments are fairly flexible but also subject to injury when overused. The healing process for strained or torn ligaments and tendons is relatively slow as compared to the healing of a broken bone.

Joints are body parts that interact with the muscles to produce movement and are composed of bone, cartilage, tendons, and ligaments. There are two kinds of joints: ball-and-socket joints, such as the hip and shoulder, and hinge joints, such as the knee and ankle.

Cartilage acts as a shock absorber for the body between the bones and is composed of collagen, a protein also found in bone. It is primarily found at the ends of bones where the joints connect. Cartilage keeps the bones from moving against each other and causing pain.

Tendons have an inner sheath that contains fluid. This fluid acts as a lubricant so tendons can slide back and forth easily. When a tendon is overworked, the inner sheath can become inflamed and sore and may fill with extra fluid; this is called tendinitis. This condition is characterized by pain in the joint and surrounding tissue.

LATERAL *and* **MEDIAL** *Sections of the Knee*

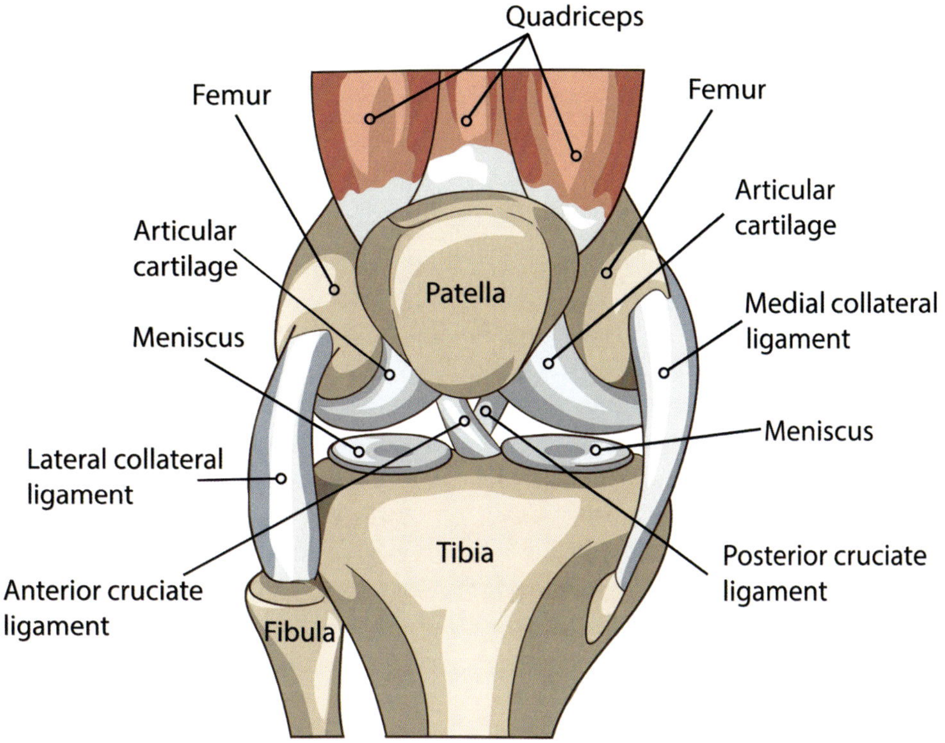

This diagram shows the different parts of the knee, including the different ligaments that connect the bones in the leg to the knee joint.

Burning Fuel

There is a complex process by which the body burns the fuel needed for energy and muscle contraction. For muscles to work at their optimum level, the body must consume various energy-giving foods, such as sugars and starches. When the food is digested, sugars and starches are converted into a substance called glycogen, or blood sugar, which is then stored and released as needed for energy.

During activity, the glycogen is broken down into lactic acid by the body; some of this lactic acid is then burned or combined with oxygen. During this process, carbon dioxide is formed, which in turn produces heat; muscles must be warm to work efficiently. A large majority of the carbon dioxide is then breathed out through the lungs, but a smaller amount is reconverted back to glycogen. This is a slow process.

Muscle Fatigue

Lactic acid is a by-product of exercise. During exercise, muscles convert glycogen (a form of glucose or sugar) to adenosine triphosphate (ATP). This is the necessary ingredient for muscles to contract. Muscle fibers convert various proteins and sugars into a compound called pyruvate. While some of this compound can be converted back to energy, most of it becomes lactic acid. Too much lactic acid can cause a muscle to become tired and stop working and can cause overall fatigue. Thus, lactic acid needs to be removed from the body following a heavy workout or a game.

The best way to do this is to continue to exercise but at a much slower pace. This is the reason many runners, after their races, continue to jog at a leisurely pace. Hockey players also do a variety of things to burn off excess lactic acid. Many ride a stationary bicycle, while others do simple exercises in the locker room. A good massage also helps because it increases blood circulation and helps clean out built-up lactic acid in the muscles.

The following exercise demonstrates how the muscles tire from excess lactic acid: Take a clothespin (the spring-loaded kind) and hold it between a thumb and index finger. Begin opening and closing the clothespin using only those fingers. After a minute of doing this, notice that you are slowing down. Count the times you are successful during the first minute and then compare it to the second minute. See if they are the same.

According to experts,

> *Odds are you slowed down significantly during your second minute [of the clothespin exercise] ... Your muscles were exercising anaerobically, drawing on their stores of glycogen to produce the ATP molecules that supply the energy they needed to contract. As the glycogen ran out, your muscles ran low on ATP and their ability to contract decreased.*[1]

1. Quoted in Science of Hockey, "Fitness," Exploratorium: The Museum of Science, Art and Human Perception. www.exploratorium.edu/hockey/fitness2.html.

Another way the body provides quick energy is the breakdown of phosphorus compounds in the muscle tissue. One of these compounds is adenosine triphosphate (ATP). This particular compound is responsible for quick energy and strong muscle contractions. If the body did not have this compound readily available, people could not participate in sports that require sudden bursts of energy.

The Results of Exercise

Ice hockey players, along with other athletes, must keep their muscles and support system working efficiently. Their bodies, therefore, need exercise. Exercise helps to strengthen the muscles and keeps a person fit to play strenuous sports, such as hockey. Scientists compare exercising to what happens when an automobile driver steps on the accelerator to make the car go. The fuel injectors feed more energy to the engine and, as a result, the engine goes faster. This process also occurs during exercise as the blood vessels carry oxygen and energy, in the form of glucose, to the muscles. According to Craig Freudenrich, PhD, "In strenuous exercise, just about every system in your body either focuses its efforts on helping the muscles do their work, or it shuts down. For example, your heart beats faster … so that it can pump more blood to the muscles, and your stomach shuts down … so that it does not waste energy that the muscles can use."[58] Scientists have determined that a working muscle can take oxygen out of the blood three times more efficiently than resting muscles. The more oxygen that reaches a muscle, the more effective and active that muscle becomes.

The key organ in this process is the heart, a hollow pump made of muscle. Its function is to pump blood throughout the body. Blood travels from the heart to every organ and tissue in the body through a system of blood vessels. As blood passes through the right side of the heart, it is oxygenated, or replenished with oxygen, when it passes through the lungs. The blood is then pumped out to the rest of the body. The average person's heart is about the size of a closed fist and beats about 60 to 100 times a minute during resting periods. During high performance activities, such as ice hockey, that rate can increase to more than twice its normal rate, thus providing more oxygen to the muscles. During training, ice hockey players concentrate on improving their endurance on the ice. Thus, an effort is made to increase cardiovascular output.

Aerobic and Anaerobic Exercise

The body has two energy systems that are used during exercise or activity: the anaerobic system and the aerobic system. The anaerobic system does not require oxygen; the word anaerobic means "without oxygen." Fitness experts Jen Mueller and Nicole Nichols explained, "Anaerobic exercise is short-lasting, high-intensity activity, where your body's demand for oxygen exceeds the oxygen supply available. Anaerobic exercise relies on energy sources that are stored in the muscles and … is not dependent on oxygen."[59] This kind of exercise utilizes the high-energy stores of chemicals, such as ATP, that are necessary for muscle contraction. This kind of exercise is crucial for the typical hockey player who tends to be on the ice for short periods of time, followed by several minutes of rest. These shifts tend to be anaerobic in nature. Twist explained, "The anaerobic energy system fuels most intense game efforts. High-speed breakaways, stop-and-start penalty killing, bodychecking, races for loose pucks, shooting, and full-intensity shifts rely on anaerobic conditioning."[60]

The other kind of exercise or activity utilizes the aerobic system, which is a system that relies on oxygen for energy. The purpose of aerobic training is to push the body to extend its capabilities, especially cardiovascular and respiratory output. Hockey players, in particular, need increased aerobic capacity to perform; it is essential that enough oxygen is available to the muscles and tissues throughout a hockey game. Aerobic endurance helps players recover between shifts so that they can perform at the same level throughout the game. Swimming, running, and other active sports are considered aerobic.

Professional athletes use both of these forms of exercise to keep themselves in shape during the season as well as the off-season.

Indian field hockey player Sardara Singh is shown here working out before a team practice at the National Stadium in New Delhi, India. All kinds of hockey players train during the off-season so they are in peak shape during the season.

Stretching Exercises

It is important for athletes at all levels to warm up and stretch prior to action. In the book, *Kids' Hockey: The Parents' Guide*, Gary Abraham wrote, "Muscles that are well stretched are less prone to injury and can work better, which translates into better performance."[1]

Abraham and other physicians recommend several different stretching exercises for hockey players. The most important are leg stretches. A groin stretch is accomplished by keeping the feet together and the back straight while pressing the knees toward the ground. The hamstring stretch involves reaching as far as possible toward the toes of the opposite foot, then repeating it on the other side. The calf stretch is done leaning against a wall with the head up and the back straight; one foot is kept close to wall while the other is slid as far out as possible without taking either foot off the ground.

The quadriceps muscle, the large muscle connecting the thigh to the hip, is also important to hockey players. To stretch this large muscle, an athlete should grasp the foot while standing and pull gently toward the buttocks. The exercise is then repeated on the other side.

A hip stretch is accomplished from a squatting position; one knee is bent forward toward the chest, while the other leg is extended as far as possible behind the knee on the ground. Finally a torso stretch can be done to work the upper body and trunk of the body. A hockey stick (or other sports equipment, such as a golf club or baseball bat) is placed across the shoulders and then rotated left and right with the upper body. Hold each stretch for a few seconds to stretch the torso muscles.

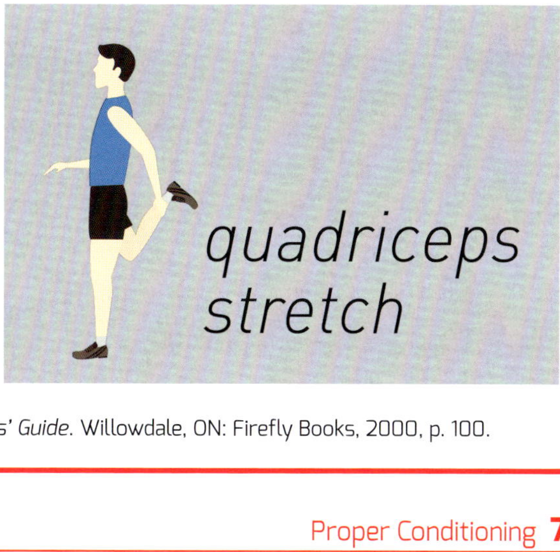

1. Gary Abraham, *Kids' Hockey: The Parents' Guide*. Willowdale, ON: Firefly Books, 2000, p. 100.

Pre-Play Preparation

Prior to the beginning of any hockey game, players focus on warming up. Allan M. Levy and Mark L. Fuerst, authors of *Sports Injury Handbook*, wrote, "Warm-up means warming up muscle fibers … The warmer muscle fibers get, the softer and more fluid they become. They are then able to stretch more easily and to contract more rapidly. The faster a muscle contracts, the stronger it is."[61]

Part of this warm-up includes exercising, which generally begins with upper and lower body stretches. Spectators to hockey games often see the players on the ice stretching leg and hip muscles, as well as rotating their shoulders and necks. Stretching in this manner is important in helping to prevent torn muscles.

In addition to stretching, players also skate as fast as they can down the length of the rink. They also practice skating backward and making sharp turns in all directions. These turns are especially important since during a game players will need to turn right and left while skating forward and backward. This ability to change direction quickly and efficiently is called agility. These drills also improve a player's balance and coordination. Fitness experts believe that coordination and balance are as important as speed in a player's agility.

Players also practice these skills during practice sessions between games. During these sessions, players participate in various speed and skating drills. They are asked to line up along one end of the ice and then skate forward as fast as possible toward the other end. They will then stop quickly and immediately sprint back to where they started. These bursts are done several times during practice. This kind of aerobic exercise is crucial for conditioning the heart and lungs for the intense bursts of speed and energy that are required during an actual game.

The drills and warm-up exercises also hone a hockey player's skills. Sean Rossiter and Paul Carson, authors of the book *Hockey The NHL Way: The Basics*, wrote, "The key to better skating is to build strength in your body's core and the muscles that radiate from there … Increased strength enables you to adopt a lower stance on the ice, use your skate-blade edges better, and get full thrust from every power stroke."[62]

Hockey players can be seen warming up on the ice before each game. They do specific stretches and drills to help them perform at their peak and avoid injury.

Year-Round Training

Most ice hockey players work hard during the off-season to keep in good shape. Mangi, Jokl, and Dayton wrote, "Hockey players must train year-round to maintain baseline fitness, so they'll be ready to get into shape for the hockey season."[63]

Hockey players are encouraged to stay active during the off-season. Many play soccer, run, or cycle to stay fit. The majority of players also continue their regular season conditioning routine by lifting weights, riding a stationary bicycle, and running. Most exercise experts believe that an effective ice hockey training plan for the off-season should include a combination of strength and muscle building, as well as anaerobic and aerobic exercise.

Strength training is an important component in off-season training programs. As hockey players lift weights, their primary concern is muscle strengthening. According to sports fitness experts, "A physiological analysis of any game … will confirm that most athletes require explosive power, muscular endurance, maximal strength or some combination of all three in order to excel."[64]

The Swiss women's ice hockey team is shown here warming up before a game at the 2014 Winter Olympics in Sochi, Russia.

Power Play

During intermissions, a player's gloves must be dried out because of intense sweating during the game.

The Water Debt

Off-season and other conditioning can only do so much in preparing a hockey player for the rigors of the long season. A player can be in the best possible shape and still face problems on the ice. One of those problems is dehydration.

As muscles become more active, more chemical energy is transferred into heat and other forms of energy. The increased circulation of blood to the skin produces sweat, which helps keep the body cool. This water, called the water debt, must be replenished by drinking sufficient liquids to replace the chemicals lost. Dehydration can actually lead to injury. Mike Fabbro explained, "Even mild dehydration will have a negative effect on physical performance. Dehydration means that your body's blood volume is decreased, which affects its ability to fuel muscles."[65]

Hockey players can be seen drinking water and other nutritional drinks during their time off the ice during games; goaltenders keep a water bottle on top of the net to replace their fluid loss. It is important for all athletes, professional and amateur, to drink lots of water and other fluids during any exercise or exertion that produces perspiration.

Hockey players, despite playing on cold ice, sweat profusely. Their time on the ice is intense and characterized by fast skating and lots of action. Players often leave the ice with perspiration dripping down their faces.

It is important for hockey players to stay hydrated and replace their fluid loss during an intense game.

Professor Lawrence Spriet of the Department of Human Health and Nutritional Sciences and graduate students Matthew Palmer, Mark Linseman, and Heather Logan at University of Guelph, conducted a study in February and March 2010 to test dehydration in hockey players. Their study involved 16 volunteers who played for 70 minutes once a week over an 8-week period. A few of the players' heart rates and core temperature increased at only 1 percent dehydration. "Even in a well-trained person who is well-adapted to handle the heat that comes with exercise, if you let yourself get dehydrated, it compromises that system,"[66] Spriet said.

Further research found that the majority of athletes became severely dehydrated during a 60-minute hockey game. Symptoms of dehydration include muscle cramps, weak and rapid heartbeat, shallow breathing, and nausea.

To prevent these symptoms, players sometimes take extreme measures to prevent dehydration. Most players drink water, sports drinks, and other fluids. In 2011, a new drink called Biosteel was developed by NHL trainer Matt Nichol. According to writer James Mirtle, "What started as a 'little pink drink'—a mix of amino acids and electrolytes that Nichol cooked up … finally began to catch on in a big way after [New Jersey Devils player Mike] Cammalleri first tried it three years ago."[67]

A Balanced Diet

In addition to conditioning and hydration, proper nutrition is also part of the preparation for a long hockey season. Most athletes require a higher energy or caloric intake than the average person. Levy and Fuerst explained, "To support training, performance and health, you should eat a balanced diet of low-fat, moderate-protein, high carbohydrate foods and beverages."[68] The diet should be accompanied by plenty of fluids.

The three basic sources of nutrients for the body are carbohydrates, fats, and proteins. Carbohydrates are made up of sugars, while fats contain a high number of calories for the production of energy. Proteins are made up of a long chain of amino acids that provide further energy. Most nutritionists believe that anyone can obtain the proper nutrients from a good diet without the need for protein, vitamin, or mineral supplements.

Some hockey players eat a high-carbohydrate diet two to three days before a game in a practice called carbohydrate loading. Simple carbohydrates are made up of sugars, such as the ones found in candy. Although athletes avoid candy, they do ingest larger than usual amounts of complex carbohydrates, such as those found in breads and pastas. Consuming a high-carbohydrate diet has been found to improve endurance. Carbohydrates are also essential for the refueling of muscles, as are proteins.

Any meal on the day of a game must be consumed several hours in advance of taking the ice. The reason for this is that the stomach needs an adequate blood supply to digest food. During a game, the body's internal control system redirects the blood flow from the stomach to other parts of the body. If a game is particularly long, players will occasionally consume energy bars during breaks in the action to increase energy.

Calories, a measure of energy, are used to measure the energy content of foods as well as the energy used by the body to perform certain activities. Thus, nutritionists can advise that running a certain distance will burn off a certain number of calories. The average inactive person requires approximately

An Old Science with New Popularity

The field of sports medicine has grown since the latter half of the 20th century. This is due to several factors, the most important of which is that more people are engaging in amateur athletics and weekend sports. Most specialists agree that untrained athletes are most likely to get hurt. In addition, professional athletes today compete at a higher level than in the past. Sports medicine professionals are in great demand because of both groups of athletes.

Sports medicine is not a new science. In fact, it was practiced more than 4,000 years ago in Egypt. In 1898, around the time of the renewal of the ancient Olympic Games, the first English textbook on sports medicine was published. The United States formed the American College of Sports Medicine in 1954. In the early 21st century, nearly every college and professional sports team had their own sports medicine physician.

Sports medicine physicians specialize in joint injuries, orthopedics (bones), or kinesiology for muscles and movement. Podiatrists treat injuries to the feet, and physical therapists use exercise and other healing techniques to help rehabilitate injured muscles and bones. Acupuncture, an ancient form of Chinese healing that uses needles inserted into key body parts, is also a form of sports medicine, as is chiropractic manipulation and realignment.

Many injured professional athletes are treated by a team of specialists to ensure they are in the best possible physical condition when returning to the playing field or hockey rink. They are aided in their return by hundreds of thousands of dollars worth of equipment that is not available to the amateur.

1,700 calories a day. Caloric intake must be increased to allow for any additional physical exercise. An endurance athlete or a professional athlete may require as many as 6,000 calories a day.

Trainers and Massage Therapists

Hockey team trainers are responsible for keeping the players in peak condition. For most hockey players, the team trainer is the person they need the most when injured or facing a long rehabilitation after an injury. In addition, the trainer is responsible for taping various parts of a player's body before games in an effort to protect knees, ankles, and other body parts from extra wear and tear.

Most teams also have massage therapists available before, during, and after a game. These therapists rub aching muscles in an effort to keep players on the ice longer. Massage therapy, which not only relaxes the muscle, but also increases the oxygen flow to the area, is also an important part of the healing and rehabilitation process after injury.

Only a physician can deal with the many ailments that are associated with long-term stress on muscles, joints, and bones. These physicians can perform surgery to repair an injury or may prescribe medication to relieve pain. Sports medicine professionals are crucial in getting an injured player back into action as soon as possible. With access to the best available treatment, a player benefits substantially and loses less ice time.

Good conditioning, a proper diet, and hydration can all improve a player's performance and health. Twist summarized, "Today, the new edge comes from adopting a training style aimed at increasing transference to on-ice actions, directly affecting on-ice abilities and driving hockey conditioning to new levels."[69]

Chapter 6

Future of Hockey

Within the last decade, hockey has gone through some revolutionary changes because of technology. Training and injury prevention are two major areas of interest athletes make sure to stay educated about to ensure they can perform at peak levels. Out of all the latest innovations, some may seem unusual, but these new tools are proven to enhance players' natural athletic abilities and prevent injuries, which otherwise could keep them from playing an entire season.

At the inception of hockey and many years after, several athletes and coaches did not even consider the idea of injury prevention. Nowadays, it is taken much more seriously to better maintain the health and longevity of the players.

ARPwave

The ARPwave machine, which is a system using bioelectrical current and active range-of-motion exercise techniques, caught the attention of NHL players looking to speed up their recoveries, prevent future injuries, and amp up their training. ARP, which stands for Accelerated Recovery Performance, works as a form of neuro-therapy used to pinpoint the origin of an injury, not just relieve the symptoms. Approximately 75 NHL players use the ARPwave and include it in their daily training routines.

Denis Thompson, founder and CEO of ARPwave said, "The first thing we test with clients is to see if the nervous system is firing properly … Then we get rid of the inflammation that is causing the compensation patterns. The third step is performance training."[70]

This small, box-shaped machine, which has been approved by the U.S. Food and Drug Administration (FDA), has assisted hockey players with knee, ankle, and several other injuries in recuperating and returning to the ice much quicker than they expected. It also has a 95 percent success rate in helping athletes in eliminating pain, restricted range of motion, and inflammation.

Jim Reger, who analyzes players' diagnoses and gives them rehab and training programs to follow, said, "With the ARP we can diagnose where the weak muscle is, and nine out of 10 times it is in another area, which means that is also where the compensation is … The ARP allows us to simultaneously diagnose where the inflammation and hot spot are."[71]

NHL player T.J. Oshie uses the ARPwave machine when he is working out, warming up before games, recovering after games, and even when he is sleeping. In 2010, Oshie rented an ARP after he broke his ankle in and used the machine as part of his rehab. He was back on the ice in January 2011, a month earlier than expected.

The Washington Capitals' Jay Beagle used the machine after he broke his hand. After using the machine, he said it seemed to work, but he was still a bit skeptical.

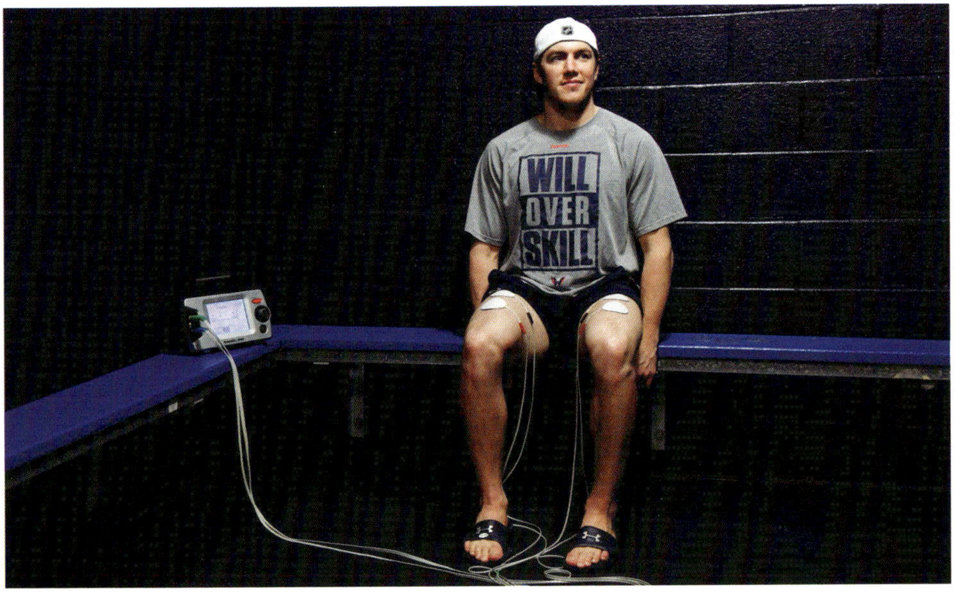

T.J. Oshie is shown here hooked up to the ARPwave, which improves a player's recovery time from an injury.

Research on the ARP conducted at the University of Hawaii medical school concluded that the machine improved quadriceps strength after ACL surgery, which can be a prolonged injury for hockey players to overcome.

Jon Bottoms, a physical therapist at TRIA Orthopaedic Center in Minnesota, said, "A lot of it is the anecdotal evidence that the players really, really stand by it and say, 'This seems to give me an edge' … If they feel that ARP gives them that, that's beneficial to them … I haven't seen any negative effects, so if I have an athlete that says, 'I want to do ARP,' I would never say, 'I don't think you should do that.'"[72]

Wearable Technology

One of the most current innovative technological advances in hockey is the addition of wearable technology. This new technology, which tracks every move a player makes, was first implemented into players' gear to give insight into their health data as a way to reduce potential injuries. Now, not only does it help players avoid injury, but it also helps them improve their athletic skills.

During the 2015 All-Star Game, the NHL put tracking devices on each player's jersey and in the puck. Statistics taken from tracking devices such as these allow players and coaches to get a better idea of a specific player's game-play technique and performance.

Q-Collar

Hockey players are known for taking blows to the head and suffering concussions. Since this is a common injury, all players are required to wear protective headgear. This consists of a helmet with a strap, and can sometimes be paired with an optional face cage or visor. Players are also told to wear neck guards and shoulder pads, but not all leagues require them. Over the years, it has been debated whether leagues such as the NHL should become stricter about mandatory protective gear and their treatment of players' concussions.

A few companies have produced wearable technology that may make a difference in helping to prevent concussions and brain injuries in hockey players. The Connecticut-based company Q30 Innovations has invented a device called the Q-Collar, which was made to help prevent the brain from moving within the skull as a player sustains a blow to the head. It gently compresses the jugular vein to mildly increase blood volume in the cranium, creating a "tighter fit" of the brain inside the skull. This action is supposed to reduce "slosh," in other words, the twisting and slamming of the brain against the skull's interior walls, which is one cause of mild traumatic brain injury (mTBI), or concussion.

"Basically you're putting a kink in the hose on the outflow," said Gregory Myer, Director of Research for the Division of Sports Medicine at Cincinnati Children's Hospital Medical Center. "What that immediately does is create a backfill in the brain and increase that blood volume."[73]

Myer conducted a study involving 15 youth hockey players through half a season to test the device's effectiveness. Results from the study, published in the journal *Frontiers in Neurology* in June 2016, showed no statistically dramatic changes in the players' brains after using the Q-Collar. However, for the players that did not use the Q-Collar during the study, changes in their brains during pre-season and mid-season tests did occur. A later study, published in the *British Journal of Sports Medicine*, of 42 high-school football players over an entire season showed similar results.

"Changes indicate alterations in the tissue and the axons that could represent brain injury," Myers said. "What we saw was that those boys that wore the collar did not have significant changes in the structural component of their brain, whereas those that didn't wear the collar, we did see a significant change."[74]

The Q-Collar is still awaiting approval from the FDA, but Myers believes after more research, future use of the device appears hopeful.

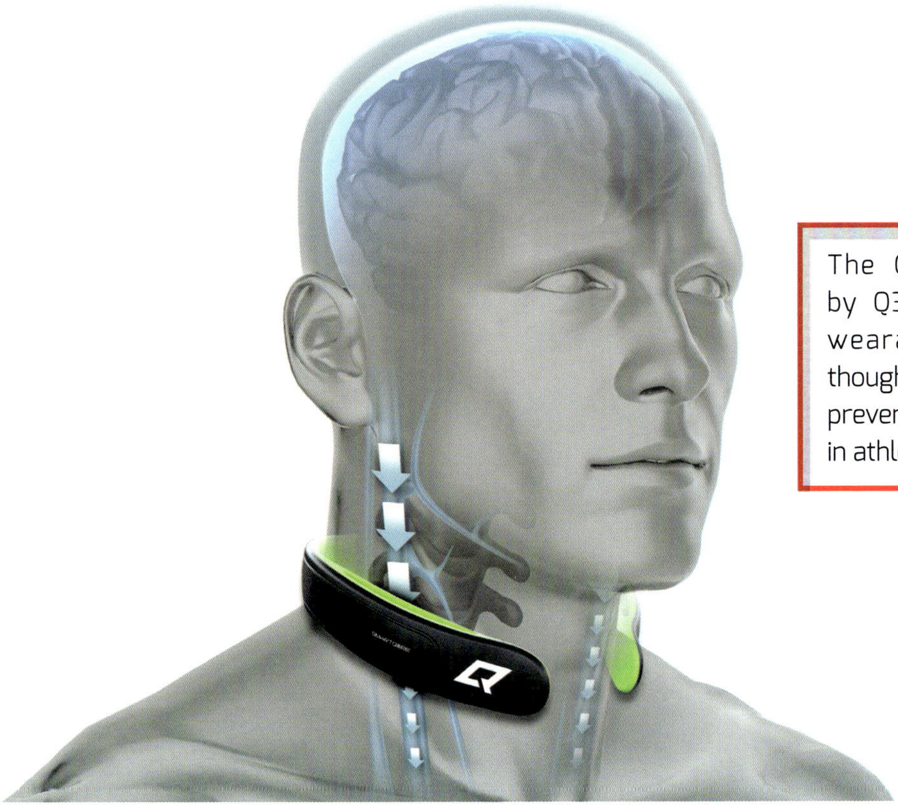

The Q-Collar created by Q30 Innovations is wearable technology thought to be useful in the prevention of concussions in athletes.

Bauer RE-AKT 75 Hockey Helmet

Researchers at the Virginia Tech-Wake Forest School of Biomedical Engineering and Sciences created another new wearable called Bauer RE-AKT 75, otherwise known as the Bauer helmet. This new helmet is another promising addition with the intent to help prevent hockey players from suffering brain injuries.

After being put to the test, the helmet received 3 out of 5 stars and was rated the highest out of all the other hockey helmet models tested. These ratings are based on which helmets will best reduce the chances of concussion for an athlete. These tests included 1,800 impact tests on 38 helmets, many of which have been available for more than 2 years.

"The Bauer RE-AKT 75 did the best job of managing impact energy and lowering head acceleration of all the hockey helmets we've tested to date," said Steve Rowson, director of the Virginia Tech Helmet Laboratory. "While there is still room for improvement, this places the new Bauer hockey helmet at the very top of our hockey helmet ratings."[75]

The Hockey Summation of Tests for the Analysis of Risk (STAR) evaluation system was implemented in April 2015. One of the main factors of criteria these helmets are tested on include whether they work to reduce linear and rotational acceleration of the head, which can be a major cause of concussion.

NHL Concussion Lawsuit

The NHL is currently facing a class-action lawsuit over their possible mishandling of players' concussions, many of which went untreated. The list of players who have filed lawsuits began with 10 in 2010, and it has now risen to more than 100. Several former NHL players, who experienced concussions during their time playing with the league, have come forward claiming the league did not do enough to ensure their safety. These players also feel the NHL should be partly responsible for the symptoms they are facing today or may face in the future. Some of these symptoms, which are related to a degenerative disease called chronic traumatic encephalopathy (CTE), include dementia, aggression, depression, and suicidal thoughts. A list of former hockey players including Bob Probert, Reg Fleming, Rick Martin, Steve Montador, Larry Zeidel, and Derek Boogaard died from complications linked to CTE.

A 2014 study titled *Concussions in the NHL: A Narrative Review of the Literature* uncovered that there were an average of 64 concussions per year in the league. During the

2014 hockey season, there were 53 reported concussions, which was an improvement from the 78 reported 2 years before.

In several instances, hockey players lose count of how many hits they have taken to the head, and this can lead to dangerous consequences and undiagnosed concussions. This lack of monitoring concussions can affect the future performance of these players and their health in the long run.

In a previous study regarding concussions in the NHL, completed in 2011, researchers discovered 559 physician-diagnosed concussions over 7 consecutive seasons. While this is a high number, there are still a good amount of concussions that slip through the cracks, which means the actual number of hockey players who suffered concussions during this time is most likely significantly higher.

Kari Lehtonen of the Dallas Stars is shown here injured with a concussion during a game against the Minnesota Wild in 2014.

"It is great to see a leading company like Bauer step-up and design an improved hockey helmet," said Stefan Duma, head of the Department of Biomedical Engineering and Mechanics. "The Hockey STAR system provides companies with the engineering foundation needed to optimize their helmet's performance."[76]

This rating system aims to provide consumers with independent data gathered on the different helmets that are on the market so they can make more informed decisions when purchasing helmets, and to provide helmet manufacturers with impact performance criteria they can use to improve future helmet designs.

Hockey players' helmets and face guards help to shield them from flying pucks.

Shockbox Helmet Sensor

Another useful wearable developed to protect players from serious concussions is the Shockbox helmet sensor. This sensor created by the Washington-based company i1 Biometrics, which focuses on sports and military markets, is one of their leading products among hockey players.

The purpose of this sensor is to inform players and coaches of how many hits to the head a certain player has experienced during a game and the severity of those hits. Once they are informed of this, they can then make a wise decision on whether that player can continue to play or if it is in the player's best interest to sit out of the game to prevent further injury.

"I am a travel hockey coach and I wish that all of my players were using this device on their helmets," wrote Kevin S., a hockey coach from Illinois, in a Shockbox testimonial. "Knowing through good science when a player should or should not be playing is utterly invaluable. I take the safety of the players under my charge very seriously, and worry that there are times I've made a poor judgment that will hurt a child unintentionally."[77]

The Shockbox helmet sensor tracks the amount of hits to the head a player has endured.

Another feature of the Shockbox sensor is that it connects directly to Apple, Android, or Blackberry devices. This updates parents and coaches immediately about their child's safety.

"The Shockbox Impact Alert Sensor is like having a trained and unbiased set of eyes looking after your child for a potential concussion while on the ice," said Michelle D., a parent of a hockey player in Massachusetts. She added,

> *As a mom who sustained a TBI, I learned firsthand the effects a concussion can have. Having a Shockbox on my son's helmet has given me the confidence that if/when he sustains a questionable fall/hit I do not have to worry about the coach or referee missing it. Literally, I have the knowledge in the palm of my hands … I think of it as just another piece of hockey equipment.*[78]

Injury Prevention Systems

Injury is generally part of a hockey game, no matter how hard one tries to prevent it. While there are new technological tools athletes can use to better avoid serious injuries, there is always the chance one may fall victim to an injury.

One program that effectively tests an athlete's performance is the Athlete Optimization System developed by the sports and data technology company Kitman Labs in 2012. This system tracks an athlete's responses to physical and mental stress endured during training and exercise at strenuous levels of high competition. The results from this test give coaches and trainers a better idea of how to structure an athlete's training or recovery regimen, especially if they are still on the mend from previous injury, and it also helps them to avoid further injury.

"Nobody has ever tried to combine all types of tech knowledge in terms of injuries – training, recovery, etc.," said Stephen Smith, the founder and CEO of Kitman Labs. "The question is, how can we better manage our athletes? There is so much information available, but a lack of turning that information into preventative knowledge and decision making in real-time."[79]

Variables considered when testing athletes using the Athlete Optimization System include "amount of gym repetitions, information on acceleration and deceleration, psychological factors (sleep, stress, mood, well being), biomechanical response, fatigue, soreness and methods of recovery that pertain to each individual athlete."[80]

"It's not just about being able to track what these athletes do, it's about tracking how they respond" Smith said. "The greatest thing about this system is that it continues to learn over time. For each athlete, teams can ensure that they can push themselves forward and get bigger, faster and stronger, while managing injury risk."[81]

Twenty-five percent of the injuries that occur during the Olympics generally are linked to how those athletes train leading up to the event. Kitman Labs worked with the Irish Men's National Hockey Team before the Rio 2016 Olympic Summer Games to help prepare their bodies and proactively prevent injury. Although these were not ice hockey players, they prepared with the same level of intensity for Olympic competition.

"These athletes are walking a tightrope," Smith explained. "They spend four years of their lives building up for this competition. If they stay away for too long, or train too little, they may not be able to compete at the highest level. It's about trying not to fall on either side of the tightrope."[82]

Staying Informed on New Technologies

As the world of hockey continues to evolve with advanced technology for training and injury prevention, hopefully the amount of injuries will decrease. With the advanced knowledge available at players' fingertips, it is important for them to be aware of the technology out there that can help them stay healthy, increase their stamina and endurance as athletes, and prevent injuries.

Compared to how hockey started out, with most players playing hockey without any mandatory protective gear, the game has become much safer for players now. However, the sport of hockey, especially in national leagues, may still have a long way to go in maintaining that safety, especially in preventing concussions in their players.

Whether or not these leagues prioritize player safety to a larger degree, the players themselves should stay informed on how to effectively train and prevent their own injuries. The game of hockey can be a violent one, and staying educated will help each player's performance and help ensure their future in the sport.

Notes

Chapter 1: Hockey: A History

1. *English Oxford Living Dictionaries*, s.v. "ice hockey," Accessed May 11, 2017. en.oxforddictionaries.com/definition/ice_hockey.
2. James Bassil, "Wayne Gretzky Interview," Askmen. www.askmen.com/celebs/interview_400/439_wayne-gretzky-interview.html.
3. Alisha Jeter, "New Course Puts Golf into Its Misty Past Sculpture of Indians Playing Shinny Will Remind Golfers of How Game Might Have Begun," *Rocky Mountain News*, July 15, 1997.
4. Gary Abraham, *Kids' Hockey: The Parents Guide*. Willowdale, ON: Firefly Books, 2000, p. 15.
5. Douglas Hunter, *A Breed Apart: An Illustrated History of Goaltending*. Chicago, IL: Benchmark, 1995, p. 18.
6. Andrea Kannapell, "Heading Slowly into the Ice Age; Women's Hockey Is Growing, if Not at Olympic Speed," *New York Times*, February 17, 1998. www.nytimes.com/1998/02/17/nyregion/heading-slowly-into-ice-age-women-s-hockey-growing-if-not-olympic-speed.html.
7. Abraham, *Kids' Hockey*, p. 17.
8. Abraham, *Kids' Hockey*, p. 17.

Chapter 2: The Physics of Hockey

9. Brandon Keim - Wired. "The Science of Hockey Ice," Gizmodo.com, June 6, 2012. gizmodo.com/5916151/the-science-of-hockey-ice.
10. Science of Hockey, "The Ice," Exploratorium: The Museum of Science, Art and Human Perception. www.exploratorium.edu/hockey/ice1.html.
11. Quoted in Brett Cyrgalis, "A Brutally Ugly Show of Hockey will go Down as Rangers Escape," *New York Post*, January 22, 2017. nypost.com/2017/01/22/a-brutally-ugly-show-of-hockey-will-go-down-as-rangers-escape/.
12. Kirsten Weir, "Hot Shots: Hockey Plays by the Rule of Physics," *Current Science*, December 12, 2008.

13. Weir, "Hot Shots."
14. Science of Hockey, "Skating," Exploratorium: The Museum of Science, Art and Human Perception. www.exploratorium.edu/hockey/skating2.html.
15. Quoted in Science of Hockey, "Skating."
16. Laura Stamm, "Good Skater or Great Skater?," LauraStamm.com, March 2008. www.laurastamm.com/tips/GoodSkaterorGreatSkater.htm.
17. Laura Stamm, "Circle Physics and Speed in Crossovers," Laura Stamm Power Skating, November 2004. www.laurastamm.net/power-skating-crossovers.aspx.
18. Stamm, "Circle Physics and Speed in Crossovers."

Chapter 3: Shooting and Stopping the Puck

19. Quoted in "Hockey Quotes," Topend Sports. www.topendsports.com/sport/icehockey/quotes.htm.
20. "Behind the Scenes Series—Frozen Biscuits," NHL Officials Association, Accessed May 17, 2017. www.nhlofficials.com/es3552/cat127/behind-the-scenes-series-frozen-biscuits.
21. "Hockey Stick Lie—Get Your Angles Right for Better Puck Control," HockeyStickExpert.com. hockeystickexpert.com/hockey-stick-lie-better-puck-control.
22. Angus McLean, "The Effect of Shape on the Flexibility of a Hockey Stick," The Physics of Hockey, November 16, 2008. www.thephysicsofhockey.com/documents/shape.pdf.
23. "Hockey Stick Flex: Produce Better Shots with the Right Flex/Stiffness," HockeyStickExpert.com. hockeystickexpert.com/hockey-stick-flex/.
24. Science of Hockey, "Shooting the Puck," Exploratorium: The Museum of Science, Art and Human Perception. www.exploratorium.edu/hockey/shooting1.html.
25. Weir, "Hot Shots."
26. Weir, "Hot Shots."
27. "Science of NHL Hockey: Projectile Motion," NBC Learn video, 5:34. Air Date: January 25, 2012. www.nbclearn.com/nhl/cuecard/56639.
28. "Science of NHL Hockey: Projectile Motion," NBC Learn.
29. Science of Hockey, "Making Saves," Exploratorium: The Museum of Science, Art and Human Perception. www.exploratorium.edu/hockey/save1.html.

30. Charles Q. Choi, "Key to Hockey Goalie Success Discovered," Live Science, October 26, 2006. www.livescience.com/health/061026_hockey_goalie.html.
31. Choi, "Key to Hockey Goalie Success Discovered."
32. Don Brennan, "Ottawa Senators Goalie Craig Anderson is in 'the Zone.' Ottawa Sun, January 12, 2014. www.ottawasun.com/2014/01/12/ottawa-senators-goalie-craig-anderson-in-the-zone.

Chapter 4: Avoiding Injuries

33. "Ice Hockey Injuries," Sports Injury Clinic, Accessed May 18, 2017. www.sportsinjuryclinic.net/sports-specific/ice-hockey-injuries.
34. Elizabeth Quinn, "Essential Ice Hockey Safety Equipment and Gear," verywell, updated April 21, 2016. www.verywell.com/essential-ice-hockey-safety-equipment-and-gear-3120419.
35. Elizabeth Quinn, "Essential Ice Hockey Safety Equipment and Gear."
36. Hunter, *A Breed Apart*, p. 8.
37. "What is Nike Dri-Fit?," Nike, 2017. help-en-us.nike.com/app/answer/a_id/204.
38. Abraham, *Kids' Hockey*, p. 93.
39. Hunter, *A Breed Apart*, p. 123.
40. Quoted in Ed Miller, "Jacques Plante: The Man in the Fiberglass Mask," The Hockey Writers, November 15, 2012. thehockeywriters.com/jacques-plante-the-man-in-the-fiberglass-mask/.
41. Richard Mangi, Peter Jokl, and O. William Dayton, *Sports Fitness and Training*. New York, NY: Pantheon, 1987, p. 299.
42. Allan M. Levy and Mark L. Fuerst, *Sports Injury Handbook: Professional Advice for Amateur Athletes*. New York, NY: Wiley, 1993, p. 49.
43. Mangi, Jokl, and Dayton, *Sports Fitness and Training*, p. 238.
44. Mangi, Jokl, and Dayton, *Sports Fitness and Training*, p. 238.
45. Abraham, *Kids' Hockey*, p. 106.
46. Steve Milton, "Blood on the Ice," *Hamilton Spectator*, February 16, 2008.
47. Quoted in Milton, "Blood on the Ice."
48. Sarah Larimer, "Even After Richard Zednik's Frightening Injury, Don't Expect Neck Guards in NHL," *USA Today*, February 13, 2008. usatoday30.usatoday.com/sports/hockey/2008-02-13-2026760421_x.htm.
49. Abraham, *Kids' Hockey*, p. 106.

50. "Hockey Fights and Violent Retaliation," The Sports Ethicist, December 20, 2013. sportsethicist.com/2013/12/20/hockey-fights-and-violent-retaliation/.
51. Quoted in Anthony R. Edwards, "Biomechanics Powers Ice Hockey Performance," *BioMechanics*, September 2004.
52. Quoted in Jim Ducibella, "Warriors of Ice: Why Do Hockey Players Put Their Bodies Through All the Punishment?," *Virginian Pilot (Norfolk, VA)*, March 29, 1996.
53. Nadav Goldschmied, and Samantha Espindola, "'I Went to a Fight the Other Night and a Hockey Game Broke Out': Is Professional Hockey Fighting Calculated or Impulsive?," *Sports Health* 5.5 (2013): 458–462. PMC. Web. March 15, 2017.

Chapter 5: Proper Conditioning

54. Peter Twist, *Complete Conditioning for Hockey*. Champaign, IL: Human Kinetics, 2007, p. xii.
55. Alain Haché, *The Physics of Hockey*. Baltimore, MD: Johns Hopkins University Press, 2002, p. 57.
56. Quoted in Science of Hockey, "Hockey Fitness," Exploratorium: The Museum of Science, Art and Human Perception. www.exploratorium.edu/hockey/fitness1.html.
57. Quoted in "Ice Hockey Training Section," Sports Fitness Advisor. www.sports-fitness-advisor.com/ice-hockey-training.html.
58. Craig Freudenrich, "How Exercise Works," HowStuffWorks, November 27, 2006. health.howstuffworks.com/wellness/diet-fitness/exercise/sports-physiology1.htm.
59. Jen Mueller and Nicole Nichols, "Reference Guide to Anaerobic Exercise," SparkPeople. www.sparkpeople.com/resource/fitness_articles.asp?id=1035.
60. Quoted in Twist, *Complete Conditioning for Hockey*, p. 54.
61. Levy and Fuerst, *Sports Injury Handbook*, p. 3.
62. Sean Rossiter and Paul Carson. *Hockey The NHL Way: The Basics*. Vancouver, B.C.: Greystone Books, 2006, p. 1.
63. Mangi, Jokl, and Dayton, *Sports Fitness and Training*, p. 302.
64. "Strength Training Section," Sports Fitness Advisor. www.sports-fitness-advisor.com/strengthtraining.html.

65. Mike Fabbro, "Hydration for Hockey," HockeyNow, July 22, 2014. hockeynow.ca/performance/hydration-for-hockey.
66. Quoted in Susan Bubak, "Hydration Should Be Goal of Hockey Players," University of Guelph, January 18, 2011. news.uoguelph.ca/2011/01/hydration-should-be-goal-of-hockey-players/.
67. James O'Brien, "Biosteel is Quickly Becoming NHL Players' Drink of Choice During Games," NBC Sports, August 23, 2011. nhl.nbcsports.com/2011/08/23/biosteel-is-quickly-becoming-nhl-players-drink-of-choice-during-games/.
68. Levy and Fuerst, *Sports Injury Handbook*, p. 21.
69. Twist, *Complete Conditioning for Hockey*, p. xv.

Chapter 6: Future of Hockey

70. Quoted in "Wave Of The Future," USAHockeyMagazine, Issue 2008–2009. usahockeymagazine.com/article/2008-09/wave-future.
71. Quoted in "Wave Of The Future," USAHockeyMagazine.
72. Quoted in Isabelle Khurshudyan, "'Shock value': T.J. Oshie one of roughly 75 NHL players who use electricity to stay in shape," *Chicago Tribune*, January 5, 2017. www.chicagotribune.com/sports/hockey/ct-nhl-players-arp-machine-shock-20170105-story.html.
73. Tom Taylor, "New Wearable Neck Collar Could Help Reduce Brain Injuries in Athletes," *Sports Illustrated*, June 15, 2016. www.si.com/edge/2016/06/15/concussion-prevention-technology-qcollar-neck-wearable-football-hockey.
74. Taylor, "New Wearable Neck Collar Could Help Reduce Brain Injuries in Athletes."
75. Quoted in "Bauer Releases New Helmet, Best Performance, According to Virginia Tech's Hockey Helmet Ratings," Virginia Tech, May 10, 2016. vtnews.vt.edu/articles/2016/05/0423116-engineering-hockeyhelmetratings.html.
76. Quoted in "Bauer Releases New Helmet, Best Performance, According to Virginia Tech's Hockey Helmet Ratings," Virginia Tech.
77. Kevin S., "Helmet Sensors Team Testimonials," Shockbox, www.theshockbox.com. www.theshockbox.com/helmet-sensors-team-testimonials/.
78. Michelle D., "Helmet Sensors Team Testimonials," Shockbox. www.theshockbox.com/helmet-sensors-team-testimonials/.

79. Quoted in Brian Wistreich, "Injury Prevention Technology Put To The Test During 2016 Rio Olympics," SportTechie, July 28, 2016. www.sporttechie.com/injury-prevention-technology-put-to-the-test-during-2016-rio-olympics/.
80. Wistreich, "Injury Prevention Technology Put To The Test During 2016 Rio Olympics."
81. Quoted in Wistreich, "Injury Prevention Technology Put To The Test During 2016 Rio Olympics."
82. Quoted in Wistreich, "Injury Prevention Technology Put To The Test During 2016 Rio Olympics."

Glossary

acceleration: A change in the velocity of something.

agility: The ability to change directions quickly and efficiently.

centripetal force: A force upon a body moving along a curved path that is directed toward the center of the curvature and keeps the body moving along the path.

checking: A physical action taken by a hockey player to stop an opponent from advancing down the ice or scoring.

concussion: An injury to the brain due to a blow or a fall.

crossover: The passing of the outside skate over the toe of the inside skate.

friction: A force that resists the motion between two bodies or substances in contact with each other.

goalie: The player who guards the net and tries to stop an opposing player from scoring.

inertia: Inactivity or rest.

momentum: The motion of a body.

reaction time: The time it takes a person to react to an action taken by another.

shootout: A one-on-one competition in which a player tries to score on the opposing goalie that is used to determine the winner of tie games.

slap shot: A powerful hockey shot that can propel the puck forward at great speeds.

sports medicine: A field of study and practice focused on preventing and treating sports injuries.

velocity: The rate at which an object changes its position.

vulcanization: A chemical process for converting rubber into more durable materials through the use of high pressure and temperature.

weight transfer: The transfer of weight and energy when an object's center of gravity shifts.

wrist shot: A hockey shot that is performed with the flick of the wrist. The puck is in contact with the stick blade for a slightly longer period of time and gives the player more control over the direction of the puck.

For More Information

Books

Burgan, Michael. *Miracle on Ice: How a Stunning Upset United a Country*. North Mankato, MN: Compass Point Books, 2016.

This book provides extensive details about the 1980 Winter Olympics game between the Russian and U.S. hockey teams.

O'Neil, Bill, and Ryan Black. *The Great Book of Ice Hockey: Interesting Facts and Sports Stories*. CreateSpace Independent Publishing Platform, 2017.

This book has sports trivia and exciting stories about players and games.

Parker, Madison. *Ice Hockey*. Vero Beach, FL: Rourke Educational Media, 2016.

This book provides details about ice hockey's rules and equipment.

Schwartz, Heather E. *Top Ice Hockey Tips*. North Mankato, MN: Capstone Press, 2017.

Schwartz's book provides helpful tips for young players to improve their game.

Waxman, Laura Hamilton. *Winter Olympic Sports: Ice Hockey and Curling*. Mankato, MN: Amicus Ink, 2017.

This book describes men's and women's ice hockey and curling as they are played in the Olympics.

Websites

Ice Hockey: Winter Olympic Sport
www.olympic.org/ice-hockey

This website includes sport and athlete records, events, photos, videos, and news about ice hockey at the Winter Olympics.

International Ice Hockey Federation (IIHF)
www.iihf.com

This website gives information about ice hockey around the world.

NBCLearn: Science of NHL Hockey
www.nbclearn.com/science-of-nhl-hockey

This series of videos contains extensive information on the science and math concepts involved in ice hockey and was made through a partnership with NBC Learn, NBC Sports, and the National Science Foundation.

NCAA Women's Ice Hockey
www.ncaa.com/sports/icehockey-women/nc

This website focuses on women's ice hockey at the college level.

NHL.com: Official Site of the National Hockey League
www.nhl.com

This website offers current statistics, news videos, player profiles, standings, and other information about professional hockey.

USA Hockey
www.usahockey.com

This group is the governing body for hockey in the United States.

Index

Picture Credits

Cover Joeleen Pryhitko/Getty Images; cover, pp. 1, 3, 4, 6, 25, 41, 54, 71, 86, 96, 102, 103, 105, 111, 112 (background) Ekaterina Koolaeva/Shutterstock.com; pp. 4, 6, 25, 41, 54, 71, 86 (hockey sticks) tmicons/Shutterstock.com; p. 7 SSPL/Getty Images; p. 11 Focus on Sport/Getty Images; p. 12 vasosh/iStock/Thinkstock; p. 15 Jana Chytilova/Freestyle Photography/Getty Images; p. 17 Matt Roberts/Getty Images; p. 18 Underwood Archives/Getty Images; p. 19 JUNG YEON-JE/AFP/Getty Images; pp. 22–23 Adwo/Shutterstock.com; p. 24 Yelena Rusko\Tass via Getty Images; p. 26 Rob Marmion/Shutterstock.com; p. 27 Jeanine Leech/Icon Sportswire via Getty Images; p. 29 JSlavy/Shutterstock.com; p. 31 MyImages – Micha/Shutterstock.com; p. 32 Past Pix/SSPL/Getty Images; p. 33 Dmytro Aksonov/E+/Getty Images; p. 35 Pressmaster/Shutterstock.com; p. 36 Dave Sandford/Getty Images; pp. 38, 40 Richard Wolowicz/Getty Images; p. 43 Sean Gallup/Getty Images; p. 45 katatonia82/Shutterstock.com; p. 46 Frederick Breedon/Getty Images; p. 48 Ronald Martinez/Getty Images; p. 50 ERWIN SCHERIAU/AFP/Getty Images; pp. 52, 53 Tim Clayton/TIM CLAYTON/Corbis via Getty Images; p. 55 Sergei Butorin/Shutterstock.com; p. 56 (left) Nicholas Piccillo/Shutterstock.com; p. 56 (right) Jonah_H/Shutterstock.com; p. 57 Fred Kfoury III/Icon Sportswire via Getty Images; p. 59 George Silk/The LIFE Picture Collection/Getty Images; pp. 61, 65 Harry How/Getty Images; p. 63 Alila Medical Media/Shutterstock.com; p. 68 Eliot J. Schechter/NHLI via Getty Images; p. 70 Rob Carr/Getty Images; p. 72 William N. Jacobellis/New York Post Archives / (c) NYP Holdings, Inc. via Getty Images; p. 75 Viktoriia Panchenko/Shutterstock.com; p. 78 Mohd Zakir/Hindustan Times via Getty Images; p. 79 (both) BigMouse/Shutterstock.com; p. 80 Bill Smith/NHLI via Getty Images; p. 81 JONATHAN NACKSTRAND/AFP/Getty Images; p. 82 Agris Krusts/Shutterstock.com; p. 87 Ricky Carioti/The Washington Post via Getty Images; p. 89 © Q30 Innovations, LLC; p. 91 Thomas B. Shea/Getty Images; p. 92 Bruce Bennett/Getty Images; p. 93 (top and bottom) © i1 Biometrics.

About the Author

Barbara M. Linde has written over 100 nonfiction books for children and young adults. She enjoys doing research and exploring topics firsthand, including spending time on horse ranches, holding a baby alligator, kayaking through mangrove estuaries, and watching spacecraft launches. Barbara has interviewed many experts, including astronauts, rocket scientists, geologists, historians, roller coaster designers, and military personnel. Some of her titles include: *Rocket Scientists*, *Force and Motion at the Amusement Park*, *Civil Rights Crusaders: Thurgood Marshall*, and *Behind the Scenes with Coders: Computer Network Architects*. She lives in Yorktown, Virginia, with her husband, Jeffrey, and a large personal library.